FINAL REMAINS

June 4, 1990: FBI Agents Smith and Adams, accompanied by Kentucky State Police Sergeant Fred Davidson and his search dog, arrived at the remote area of Harmon's Branch, nine miles outside of Pikeville, Kentucky. They had specific instructions about where to search for the body of twenty-seven-year-old Susan Daniels Smith, but the ravine on the side of the road was so heavily overgrown, they were useless. As their grisly work began, the men who had gone down the steep embankment all but disappeared in the thick brambles and trees.

Then, just before nightfall, one of the searchers spotted what appeared to be a human skull. Upon further scrutiny, the team uncovered the remains of the dead girl—a skeleton, the rib cage intact, partially concealed by leaves. The arm and leg bones had been shifted around, most likely by wild animals. Her jawbone lay near the skull, missing two molars.

A tiny gold chain and cross was found next to the skeleton. This was the jewelry Susan had borrowed from her sister the day she had left to meet her lover, FBI Special Agent Mark Steven Putnam, nearly one year before.

HE'S THE LAST MAN YOU'D EVER
WANT TO MEET IN A DARK ALLEY . . .

THE EXECUTIONER

By DON PENDLETON

THE FBI KILLER

APHRODITE JONES

PINNACLE BOOKS
WINDSOR PUBLISHING CORP.

For
Susan Daniels Smith

PINNACLE BOOKS

are published by

Windsor Publishing Corp.
475 Park Avenue South
New York, NY 10016

First printing: September, 1992

Printed in the United States of America

ACKNOWLEDGMENTS

All the material in this book, except for my own observations, is derived from official court records, police reports, and interviews with the persons directly concerned with the case. Because these "collaborators" are identified within the text, I will not name them here; however, I want to express my gratitude for their patient cooperation. Two friends, Edith Walker and Bonnie Butler, I do name because they personally assisted me and made my task possible. Also, I would like to single out a few people whose contributions to my work were very specific: Dr. David Wolfe, Forensic Anthropologist, Kentucky Justice Cabinet; Supervisory Special Agent James Huggins, Federal Bureau of Investigation; Major Jerry Lovitt, Commander–East Branch, Kentucky State Police, and his men; Larry Webster, whose assistance in legal matters was invaluable; Harry M. Caudill, author of *Night Comes to the Cumberlands;* Mike Sager, free-lance journalist; Lee Mueller, Eastern Kentucky Bureau Chief of the *Lexington Herald Leader;* Richard Foley, my colleague at Cumberland College; and finally, the hardworking journalists from the *Appalachian News Express* and the *Williamson Daily News,* whose reporting helped me especially in the writing of the final chapters.

Aphrodite Jones
Williamsburg, Kentucky
September, 1992

Chapter One

Freeburn sits smack in the middle of the Hatfield-McCoy historic district, and legends of murderous raids and feud-related sites are still very much alive in the memories of its inhabitants. Founded in 1911, the town was first called Liss in honor of Liss Hatfield. In 1932 it was renamed Freeburn because of the free-burning coal mined in the area. The area is hilly and rural, and the four hundred people who live there drive to Pikeville thirty miles away, or to Matewan, a few miles across the state line in West Virginia, to conduct their business. Located on the western slope of the Appalachian Range, the land is marked by the numerous small creeks and branches which drain from elevations of land averaging about fifteen hundred feet, with an average creek bottom being about seven hundred feet above sea level.

Susan Daniels was the descendant of "Devil Anse" Hatfield, the leader of the Hatfield clan, whose grave, marked by a towering Italian marble sculpture of the bearded patriarch, is located in Logan County, West Virginia. Buried with him are the reasons behind the feud, shrouded in folklore passed down for more than one hundred years. Some say the feud started over a pig that belonged to the McCoys but wound up in the Hatfields' pen. Others say the dispute stemmed from the Civil War, in which the Hatfields fought for the Confederacy and the McCoys the Union.

Whatever the reason, violence between the families began in 1882 when Devil Anse's brother, Ellison Hatfield, was stabbed two dozen times and shot in an Election Day brawl in Pike County. Devil Anse Hatfield and his clan seized the McCoys responsible for his brother's death, tying them to pawpaw trees and executing them near McCarr, a stone's throw away from Freeburn. Today, all these generations later, people growing up in the area resent having to live down the infamous reputation brought on by the bloody and abhorrent feud years. Indeed, to the modern generations fueled by an era of television and cinematic violence, the mayhem and murder committed by the feudists almost seem to be more fiction than truth.

Be that as it may, the inhabitants of Tug Valley cannot ignore their turbulent history. For decades, the Pike County Circuit Court clerk's office recorded the deaths of scores of men who were shot down annually for little or no provocation. Year in and year out the dockets were jammed with murder and manslaughter cases. Unfortunately, this violence resulted in limiting the social contacts of the region's inhabitants. It also was responsible for the exodus of the more peaceable men, who migrated in vast numbers, moving in all directions, mostly to the north, where they could find jobs. Since the violence of the feuds kept outsiders away, local people tended to seek allegiance in their own bloodlines. "Marrying close to home" became commonplace, and in Freeburn and surrounding areas, practically every creek and hollow is filled with a tangle of cousins, aunts, uncles, parents, and grandparents.

Most people who live in mining communities cannot overcome the feeling of helplessness and captivity brought on by the severe setbacks that have plagued the coal industry. Since the Great Depression, it became the norm for miners to be discharged and forced to subsist on welfare and Social Security Insurance. The residents of Appalachia have been poor for many years, and their impoverishment has resulted in apathy. They live from season to season, with little hope of change.

By the 1960's, when Susan Daniels was born, the fifth of nine children, the national census revealed that the people of eastern Kentucky had the highest birth rate in the nation, only compounding the problems of poverty in the region. Actually Susan was born in Matewan, West Virginia, but her parents moved to Barrenshea Creek, a hollow in Freeburn, when she was a baby. By the time she was old enough to be aware of her surroundings, her father, Sid Daniels, had been laid off from work because of an arm injury.

"I worked so hard in the mines to raise nine, but it wasn't enough," Sid insisted. "On Saturdays and Sundays, I would cut mining timber to make extra money, and I tore my wrists apart."

Sid Daniels worked as a coal miner for the Majestic Collier Coal Company and the Estep Coal Company for a total of eighteen years. He got black lung—a coal miner's disease which cuts off the flow of oxygen to the lungs—but because he was a cigarette smoker, he was not eligible for any compensation from the coal companies. He would have fought for it in court, but couldn't afford an attorney.

Because Sid stopped working when Susan was a young girl, all she ever knew was a jobless father, a middle-aged, ex-coal miner with a gang of "young-uns" to support. Welfare was her family's way of life. Coal miners had their eyes dimmed, their lungs filled with particles of coal dust, and their backs broken from strenuous exertion in cramped quarters, often having to work on their hands and knees. So it became more profitable for men like Sid Daniels, who were not strong enough to do that kind of heavy labor, to sit back and draw a check.

He, along with other older unemployed miners, had been driven into a trap, and the children of these miners, Susan Daniels among them, who knew welfare as the only means of survival, would turn to various means of public support in their adult lives. The vicious circle of poor educational systems, high unemployment rates, and easy governmental subsidies left people like Susan Daniels no real choices, unless, of course, they left area and friends and family behind.

"If we had grown up differently — if we had been taught pride," Susan's sister Carla once complained, "but it's always been welfare as long as I can remember. I can't remember Daddy ever working. He had Social Security Insurance, and he knew all the tricks."

Carla called their mother, Tracy, a "conveyor belt" who cranked out another kid for a little more money. But apparently Susan didn't see her that way. She loved Tracy and Sid, and she wasn't as bitter as her brothers and sisters.

"We were all going to school with old shoes and being laughed at," Carla remembers. "Daddy could have worked. He could have given us more. I mean, we had to live with two beds in each room and a black and white TV that only got three stations. Our heat came from an old coal stove. You've got to admit, that's hard to live with."

But Susan didn't seem to have that much of a need for material things in her childhood. As a girl, she had birthday parties and Christmas trees and a Bible by her bedside, and she was relatively content. Her father built the family a small wooden house at the mouth of the "holler," and the children shared bedrooms and clothes and toys. The family ate all their meals together, lining up army style, each taking as many helpings of Tracy's homemade meals as they wanted. They didn't have any of the luxuries that the "rich people" were able to afford, but no one ever went hungry or did without clothes.

That's not to say that the Daniels weren't poor. Their lives were filled with inconveniences. There were no paved roads in the hollows, no washing machines or modern appliances, and there were at least two children to a bed in the Daniels' home. Nonetheless, Susan seemed well liked and well adjusted.

"She was happy growing up. She liked

school. She'd get library books and read all the time," Sid recalls. "She liked to read, she liked to learn things. She wanted to become a secretary. She would talk about that as a child."

However, by the time she was about ten years old, things began to change for Susan. She grew dissatisfied with her lot and even though they couldn't afford it, Sid and Tracy tried to appease her. Most of the children growing up in Freeburn had to be satisfied with used clothing purchased at local yard sales, but Susan wouldn't stand for that. She wanted to shop at the stores in Matewan. She wanted respectable clothes.

"She wanted to have nice things, so we'd take her to Hopes Department Store in Matewan. Everything was cheap back then. You could get a lot for five or ten dollars," Tracy remembers. "She carried a parasol around at that age. She'd play dress-up and carry old pocketbooks around the house. She knew she had it hard here, but she had new clothes, she had her dolls, she had her tricycle, and she had her brothers and sisters. She was doing just fine."

The Daniels family spent a lot of their time just surviving during Susan's formative years. They were a self-contained bunch. Sid would raise a hog every year, which the boys would help him slaughter. He also grew fruits and vegetables, and Susan and her sisters helped Tracy can pickles, chop cabbage, pick fruits and berries, and make jelly and jam. Once a week, they'd all go to Matewan in Sid's Chevy truck to buy necessities — flour, lard, salt, soap, toothpaste, and shampoo. But life wasn't really that bad for the Daniels family. Others up in the hills had it a lot worse. It wasn't as though Susan grew up without electricity or indoor plumbing. It wasn't as though the Daniels family couldn't manage. The kids did their share of chores. The girls cleaned and dusted and folded laundry. The boys worked on the house, building and repairing things.

The Daniels children also had a good deal of innocent fun while growing up. They played hide-and-seek out in the wild virgin territory that surrounded them. They climbed up and down hills, ran across rivers on swing bridges. Tucked away from the noise and stress of urban living, they had just about all they needed right there at the mouth of Barrenshea Creek. Sid even kept a pony for the kids to ride. For Susan as a child, life in Freeburn was simple yet precious. The Tug Fork of the Big Sandy has a beauty and serenity typical of the whole isolated and untouched region, and Susan was happy to be living there.

In fact, most of the people in the Pike

her in Monroe after a trip to his sister Irene's in Princeton, West Virginia.

However Kenneth didn't make it to Monroe for some time. Evidently he wound up living with a woman in Elliston, Virginia, just outside of Roanoke, where he remained for months without ever contacting Susan. Growing impatient and uneasy, she eventually moved out of Roger's place, finding a female roommate and a job at a Kentucky Fried Chicken restaurant in Monroe. Susan was out on her own for a while, and she was scared and lonely, praying for Kenneth to appear.

Sure enough, not long after Susan moved out of Roger's place, Kenneth arrived in Louisiana. It took Kenneth a few days to decide to look Susan up; then he just popped into the fast-food place unannounced, much to her surprise.

Within hours, the two of them picked up right where they had left off in Freeburn. Susan, still in love with Kenneth, was afraid to question him about his absence, afraid to anger him in any way. She just assumed he'd been on the run from the law. At the time, she didn't comprehend that she was just a convenience for him. Kenneth was not really attracted to her. Susan's breasts weren't fully developed, she was skinny, and she was only seventeen years old, too young in his eyes. Nonetheless, within three weeks of Kenneth's arrival in Louisiana, Susan quit her job and moved in with him over at Roger's. Roger had a wife, Francis, who was a bookkeeper at a motel in Monroe, and for a while, Francis supported the four of them. It was about a month before Kenneth figured out what his next move would be. All the while, he kept in touch with his brother Roy, who lived in Freeburn, and was informed that his old pal Carl "Cat Eyes" Lockhart was about to pull off a bank robbery.

When word came that Cat Eyes and two others had robbed the Hurley Bank in Grundy, Virginia, it was front-page news. The take was three hundred eighteen thousand dollars. It was the largest bank robbery in Virginia's history, for which Lockhart subsequently received an eighteen-year prison sentence.

"It wasn't any surprise to me when I found out Cat Eyes pulled that off. I grew up with him," Kenneth says, "and Cat always wanted to rob a bank. He talked about it ever since he was a kid."

Not long after the Hurley Bank robbery, Cat Eyes pulled up at Roger's driving a new white Eldorado Cadillac. He was a fugitive on the run, and Roy Smith was with him, along for the joy ride. Susan and Kenneth were in the kitchen having coffee when Cat Eyes appeared, asking Kenneth to step into the back bedroom; he wanted Kenneth to see something. Cat Eyes opened a briefcase and showed Kenneth over a hundred thousand dollars in cash, his share of the heist. Kenneth just looked at the stacks of bills and went back into the kitchen without saying a word.

"From the minute he got there, Cat Eyes couldn't spend his money fast enough," Kenneth recalls. "He begged me to go with him to Chicago, but I wouldn't do it. He wanted to buy drugs, so he flew off and left me with the briefcase of money. It was funny because he didn't trust me. He called me just about every hour while he was gone."

Evidently Cat Eyes had reason to worry, because Susan actually tried to run off in the Eldorado with the briefcase of money while he was gone, but Kenneth was able to catch her. Cat Eyes came back from Chicago with an ounce of cocaine, which he shared with Susan and Kenneth and Roger and the rest. The group stayed "coked up" for about five days, and Cat Eyes talked about investing his money. But Kenneth couldn't get him to take any advice.

"I tried to help him. I told him to buy six trailers and rent them out so he could have an income, because the way he was spending, I knew he was going to wind up having to rob another bank and he'd get caught. The money was burning a hole in his pocket."

Clearly Cat Eyes needed to throw his money around, because up in Chicago he bought an ounce of coke, paying for it by the gram at a hundred dollars per, giving the dealer a five-hundred-dollar tip. According to Kenneth, Cat Eyes returned, bragging that he had given this girl twenty-eight hundred dollars for an ounce of cocaine which should have cost about fifteen hundred dollars. "He just wanted to impress her," Kenneth explained.

During his short stay in Louisiana, Cat Eyes found other ways to waste his money and he lost almost ten thousand dollars to Kenneth in poker games before he left, eventually making it to Hendersonville, Tennessee, taking Kenneth's brother Roy with him. While in Hendersonville, Cat Eyes spent the remainder of his hundred thousand dollars on expensive whores and drugs, which he imported from nearby Nashville. Roy later told others that Cat got "strung out" on one particular hooker, handing her twenty-five hundred dollars a day.

Just a month and a half after the bank heist, Cat Eyes landed back in Freeburn, dead broke. Within two days, the law picked him up at a bar across the river in Vulcan, West Virginia, and inside of a year, Cat Eyes was serving his sentence in a federal penitentiary.

Meanwhile, Susan and Kenneth had befriended one of Roger's neighbors in Monroe, a preacher by the name of Michael, who had been coming around regularly with his wife, Linda. Susan and Linda became fast friends, exchanging recipes and talking about their favorite soaps, about who shot J.R. on *Dallas* and little things like that. It was the easy life for Susan, and she was happy there with Kenneth, but Kenneth didn't like Louisiana. He was tired of the place. There were no drugs around, and he was bored.

When the proposition came up for Michael to take a job at a congregation in Columbus, Indiana, Kenneth jumped at the idea of moving up north with Susan. It would be closer to Kentucky, closer to Illinois. And before they knew it, all three couples, the preacher and his wife, Roger and Francis, and Kenneth and Susan, wound up moving—lock, stock, and barrel—to Columbus, Indiana.

In Columbus, Kenneth bought a trailer for sixty-five hundred dollars with the money he had hustled from Cat Eyes. Then he got himself a construction job and began putting up prefab housing, making pretty good money. Roger was selling insurance and was pulling in about five hundred dollars a week; he lived in an apartment near Kenneth. And Michael seemed to be doing well with his congregation. For a while, everything was going favorably.

However, after just a few months, Susan became restless. She wanted a faster paced life. She wanted access to drugs. She and Kenneth began arguing. When the opportunity came to move to Chicago with her sister, Christine, Susan took off and found a job as a factory worker in Cicero, Illinois, a Chicago suburb. But the job didn't work out, and Susan was fired. After that, she couldn't seem to hold any steady job. She kept moving from one factory position to another, and she eventually tired of that life. Within six months, Kenneth went up to Chicago and brought Susan back to live with him in Indiana.

Chapter Two

Throughout the summer of 1980, Susan and Kenneth spent time in Columbus with Roger, Francis, Michael, and Linda, their constant companions. If the union of Susan and Kenneth had been rocky at one time, by now things had turned around. They enjoyed each other's company, and they had their little group to keep busy. Sometimes the friends all went picnicking at a nearby lake, and the others began to notice that Susan, having blossomed into a full-grown woman, had no trouble attracting male attention, whether swimming in a bikini or walking along trails in an old T-shirt Kenneth had given her. Kenneth took Susan fishing and she was thrilled with her first catch, a carp. Life with Kenneth was starting to look really good to her.

The pair rarely argued anymore, they began attending Michael's church regularly, and they were talking about marriage. Shelby came up to visit her sister a few times, and she always filled Susan in on what was happening in

Freeburn with the rest of the Daniels family. Susan had lost touch with most of her brothers and sisters by then, but remained in contact with her parents by mail; Sid and Tracy have never owned a telephone. She believed that Kenneth was truly in love with her, and she was content, finally living a normal life.

"When I was working, she would get breakfast ready for me and then come wake me up to eat. And whenever I got home, the table was always set. She'd fix just whatever you'd want. 'Bar-b-cue' ribs, spaghetti and meat balls, and she enjoyed doing it, she was happy," Kenneth remembers. "She had the place fixed up real nice. We had pictures taken together at a studio, and Susan hung them on the walls. She had this wooden case in the living room filled with tiny crystal statues I bought her. I remember once she was real upset because she had broken one of them; it was a little mule pulling a cart. I told her not to worry about it, but she was just that way. She wanted everything perfect. She was a real good housekeeper."

While Kenneth was out laying floors and ceilings, Susan would stay at home in the trailer, building a nest for the two of them, cleaning, moving furniture around, taking care of the plants, and watching her favorite soap operas. The pair had gone shopping when she'd first gotten back and had spent over twelve hundred dollars setting up house, buying blankets, towels, sheets, dishes, and silverware at the local mall, so she had made the trailer quite comfortable.

Kenneth had a La-Z-Boy recliner. He would come home, kick off his work boots, and relax in it. Susan had covered the walls of their bedroom with fancy green fabric, and she thought her sex life was better than ever, now that she was beginning to experiment, becoming more sure of herself in bed. Kenneth said they'd planned to mirror one bedroom wall, but had never got around to it. According to him, their sexual activities needed no improvement. In public, they led a quiet life, taking long walks in the park every evening. In private, they had an active sex life, "making it" in every room in the trailer: on the bathroom sink, in the shower, on the kitchen floor, and up against the fabric-covered walls of the bedroom.

Kenneth and Susan spent a little over a year in Columbus. All along, she constantly told him that she wanted children, and just after her twentieth birthday, they agreed to take the big step. Kenneth got down on his knees and proposed in a mock fashion.

On February 5, 1981, in Columbus, Indiana, Kenneth and Susan were married.

The wedding ceremony was simple — nobody in Susan's family was contacted — just the two of them and the preacher and his wife. Susan didn't wear white or carry any flowers. In fact, they were wed in blue jeans. They didn't even go out and buy a wedding ring. Instead, they used

29

a turquoise ring Kenneth had given Susan years before.

After the ceremony, the pair went out to a nice dinner, but there was no honeymoon. Life just went on as usual. Drugs were still a part of the picture, but they were not dealing anymore. Kenneth would go to Chicago to get some coke or PCP for their own use, but that was about the extent of it. Then, about six months into the marriage, Susan became pregnant. It wasn't planned—the couple never used birth control; they used the rhythm method—but it was a welcome surprise to both of them.

"I was tickled to death that she was pregnant, and she looked great—she never got fat. She ate a lot of fruits. She had to have her fruits. Sometimes she'd send me out in the middle of the night for watermelon, cantaloupe, plums, just whatever she had a taste for," Kenneth recalls. "She looked happy all the time. All through her pregnancy, her face was glowing. We bought a crib—we had that ready—and we'd pick out names. We must have gone through twenty or thirty."

Kenneth was in the delivery room with Susan when she gave birth to their daughter, Miranda Lynn Smith, on March 25, 1982. They had taken Lamaze classes together, and the delivery went well.

But while Susan and Kenneth now seemed to have their lives on the right track, Roger and Francis weren't doing as well for themselves.

According to Kenneth Smith, while Susan was pregnant, Roger had fallen more heavily into a drug-usage pattern and had begun making more regular trips to Chicago to purchase cocaine. During this time he lost his job, and he decided he would rob a bank in Columbus, using techniques Cat Eyes had bragged about down in Louisiana. He and Francis pulled off the robbery just a few weeks after Susan gave birth to Miranda. But they were caught. Roger was pictured on the front pages of the local newspapers and was eventually sent to jail.

From that point on things started to go downhill for Kenneth and Susan. Kenneth found himself forced out of the construction business without the benefit of unemployment payments. He had fallen from the roof of a building, but was unable to get compensation, the doctors claiming he was fit to work, Kenneth insisting he wasn't. Because of the back injury he'd sustained in the fall, Kenneth began to rely heavily on pain pills, and with Roger in jail and no money coming in, he decided to move, with Susan, back to Kentucky, closer to home, closer to his former drug connections.

At first Susan and Kenneth stayed with his sister in Princeton, West Virginia. Irene was good to Susan, giving her expensive clothes and even furs that she no longer used. Susan loved Irene, and would continue to make visits to Princeton throughout her life, regardless of her problems with Kenneth. In Princeton, Susan and Kenneth were just a two-hour drive from Freeburn, and soon Susan contacted her sister, Shelby, who was now divorced from James Hardin and remarried to an older, more successful man, Ike Ward. Shelby made some calls to help Susan find housing, and by the spring of 1983, Susan and Kenneth were settled in a trailer in Majestic, Kentucky. They were renting it from Shelby's new sister-in-law. They had made the full circle. They were back home again.

No one in the Freeburn area could get over the way Susan had changed, had grown into such a beautiful young woman. Her experience of the outside world made her appear more sophisticated to the people she had left behind in Kentucky. She had lost much of her "hillbilly" accent, and she wore high heels, makeup, and the latest fashions. People hardly recognized her.

Susan Smith was complimented by everyone she met, and she relished all the attention. But being back in Kentucky posed problems for her, and life there was not as easy as she had hoped it might be. For one thing, Kenneth was still a fugitive who had to worry about being captured by the law. For another, Susan's brothers and sisters had troubles which they constantly brought to her, complicating her existence even further.

Susan was a good listener, a good shoulder to cry on, and she soon discovered that while she had been gone, a number of misfortunes had struck her siblings: her brother Lacy had slit his wrists one year at the Matewan Fair. He'd lived through it, but refused to talk much to anybody in the family afterward. Her sister Carla had been widowed at the age of twenty-one, her husband Larry having been killed in a barroom brawl in Freeburn. Another brother, Tennis, was constantly in trouble with women. Shelby, meanwhile, had dumped the two kids from her first marriage into Tracy and Sid's lap. She was trying to make a clean go of it with Ike Ward, who allegedly was not without his own problems. According to Kenneth, Ike would come up to their trailer in Majestic and fight with Susan over money. And by now, Susan had her own difficulties; she and Kenneth were back in the drug-dealing business, making routine runs to Chicago in order to support themselves and their daughter.

Not long after they arrived, Kenneth contacted Pikeville attorney Kelsey Friend, Jr., regarding his warrant of arrest and forfeited bond. Kenneth's trial date was set for June, but Friend had the trial postponed. On February 29, 1984, Kenneth Smith pled guilty to selling a quantity of PCP to Pike County Detective Leroy Weddington. He was sentenced to five years' probation for the drug-trafficking charges.

By the time of Kenneth's court appearance in 1984, family members say Susan had become thoroughly disgusted with Kenneth's drug addiction and his lies, and they were having real problems in their marriage. Kenneth refused to work and stayed away much of the time, leaving Susan with a small child to raise and no income. She finally was forced to go on welfare.

There is no record of Susan Daniels Smith ever having been charged with drug trafficking or any other criminal offense, and it must have irked her to have to constantly defend Kenneth to friends and family, who chided her for marrying an addict and a criminal, a man who would not support his family. After three years of marriage, Susan threatened to leave Kenneth, and in the fall of 1984, she moved in with Carla, who resided in Newtown, West Virginia, just outside Matewan.

Carla was still mourning the loss of her husband, Larry, and the two young women did a lot of drugs together, to drown their sorrows, according to Carla. She remembers the laughs she and Susan shared when, under the influence, Susan forgot about Kenneth and told of some of her misfortunes and adventures.

"When we were high, she always told me these big stories about city life, but I think basically when she went to those places, she was running. She just wanted to get away from Freeburn. It wasn't that she wanted the department stores and the malls, that didn't matter to her," Carla recalls. "Once she told me she went out with this guy in Chicago and he took her to this apartment that was barely furnished, and he started acting pretty strange after a while. He jumped on top of her with his clothes still on. He was smothering her, and she told me she was thinking, Oh my God, I'm going to die, this guy's going to kill me, he's going to do something crazy. But all that happened was the guy had an orgasm with his clothes on. We really laughed about that."

And in between the drugs and the laughter about men, the two sisters were both dating quite a bit. In fact, unbeknownst to Susan, Carla was seeing Kenneth Smith. She even slept with him sometime during 1984, after Susan had separated from him. Susan found that out years later in the middle of an argument and was never really close with Carla again. At one point, she got back at her by sleeping with one of her sister's boyfriends.

During the separation Susan claimed she had become involved with Marlow Tackett, a local country-music singer. Though overweight and rough looking, Tackett was able to attract women because he owned a successful nightclub. The place had a reputation for gun fights and brawls, but people from all over Pike County flocked to Marlow's, over by Harmon's Branch just outside Pikeville, and Susan spent many of her nights there.

"Susan showed me a picture of Marlow in a black cowboy hat once. It was an eight-by-ten glossy, like a picture a fan would have. She made a big deal out of him, but he never really seemed to be interested in her," Carla recalls. "She'd go down to his club, and I'd lend her things to wear. She'd get all dolled up and get one of the neighbors to give her a ride to his place. Once she wore this black leather mini dress of mine. I thought she looked really great in it, but I never could figure out what she saw in him. I never was sure she even went out with him, because, you know, Suzie would always build people up. You never knew what to believe when she told you things."

Whatever the reason, in her months of meandering, Susan was unable to find a suitable replacement for Kenneth, so she was destined to go back to him. Life was too difficult for her alone. She and Carla were stuck in Newtown without a car, and Newtown, being in the middle of former coal-camp villages with names like Cinderella, Red Jacket, and Ragland, was too far from civilization. Susan and Carla had to rely on family members and friends for transportation just to get to local grocery stores.

Kenneth would sometimes drive by with groceries for them, but Susan hated that arrangement. She was now on welfare, but was unable to collect any money from Aid to Dependent Children because Kenneth was taking care of Miranda in Majestic. Unhappy and inconvenienced, Susan missed her daughter. For her, life seemed to have no simple answers. It wasn't long before she began sleeping with Kenneth again, and soon she became pregnant. Now Susan and Kenneth had to figure out a way to support the new baby. Ironically, the solution to their problem appeared to be a divorce.

In the poverty-ridden eastern Kentucky hills, subsidies for children seem to be available only when the mother is unmarried. Matrimony precludes women from receiving Aid to Dependent Children monies unless the husband is disabled, and Kenneth Smith was not. Divorced, Susan would be eligible for state assistance. Between ADC, Social Security Insurance, and food stamps, the pair could more easily make ends meet.

Susan and Kenneth jointly petitioned for divorce on December 5, 1984. Susan was twenty-three and Kenneth was thirty. They both listed themselves as unemployed, residing in Pike County, and they claimed to have been separated since September of that year. The divorce papers originally stated that Susan Smith was not pregnant on the date of filing, but that information was amended in a petition dated March 14, 1985, when Susan told the Pike Circuit Court that she was indeed pregnant.

Kenneth and Susan Smith were awarded joint custody of their infant children, Kenneth having custody Monday through Thursday, Susan having the children Friday through Sunday. Of course, it was all just a formality. The marriage was dissolved on March 14, 1985, but

Kenneth and Susan's relationship was now going strong, and having a baby on the way insured their happiness for the time being. Miranda was two years old, just about to turn three, when she and her parents moved into a quaint two-bedroom cottage over in Vulcan, West Virginia, just across the river from Freeburn.

On August 1, 1985, their son, Brady Leon Smith, was born at the Williamson Memorial Hospital in Williamson, West Virginia. The unofficial birth certificate says the boy was born at four-thirty P.M. to "Mr. and Mrs. Kenneth Smith."

By then, Susan had fixed up their house, decorating it with curtains, silk flower arrangements, and wall hangings. The place was owned by Troy Blankenship, a gentle man who lived a few doors away. Troy collected the rent directly from the West Virginia Housing Authority, and the lease was in Susan's name. Technically, Kenneth was not supposed to be a resident, but the pair lived together as man and wife, even though they were divorced, and remained in Vulcan until the spring of 1989.

Susan requested that the house be painted pale yellow, and she did a lot of work on the inside, hanging wallpaper, painting walls, and shifting around the furniture she had purchased from neighbors and family members. It was a perfectly lovely house, save that it sat directly beside a commercial train track on which hundreds of CSX railroad cars passed day in and day out, disrupting the normal course of life. Even so, the abode was cozy enough, with a porch swing and a barbecue out front, in the back yard a gazebo which overlooked the Tug River. There was even a footbridge that ran across the river directly behind the house, connecting the Kentucky and West Virginia sides of the Tug.

The Smiths had about an eighth of an acre of land to call their own, but oddly enough, they rarely went outdoors. They had no furniture in the gazebo by the river, and little lawn furniture except for the swing on the porch. Only the children spent time in the yard, playing on the swing set Susan had managed to purchase secondhand from somebody in Freeburn. The place was heated by a wood- and coal-burning stove, so there was always a pile of coal in one corner of the yard. Susan warned her children to stay away from it. She didn't want them looking dirty like so many of the kids in Vulcan. She wanted her children to grow up with a sense of pride, and she made them think their home provided everything life had to offer.

But she felt isolated and was edgy about living in Vulcan. Though she seems to have been kind and generous — she gave away clothes to her friends, had her neighbors over for dinner, and brought gifts to all of her relatives and friends during the holiday season — by this time, Susan was not happy with her life.

According to her family and friends Susan was a genuinely nice person. Perhaps, because of her generosity and her sense of humor, no one around her realized just how unsettled she was emotionally. After all, Susan was very careful about her appearance, sacrificing a great deal to buy stylish clothing, despite her troubles at home. And at age twenty-five, Susan was adding blond highlights to her brown hair and was sporting a tan which she worked on at nearby tanning salons.

With Kenneth being gone much of the time, off with his drug-dealer friends, it wasn't long before Susan started to look around for a new man. After all, she and Kenneth weren't technically married, and she had heard rumors of his sleeping around. She began having one-night stands here and there to fill the void and ease the anger in her heart. Most nights he was out gambling, and since he refused to contribute any money for groceries and other necessities, when he was home, the pair argued bitterly, Susan sometimes calling the police to report a family skirmish. Corporal Roby Pope of the West Virginia State Police knew the Smiths well.

"Susan would call here and report a robbery or a beating, and we'd send somebody down there, but there was never anything we could do about it," Pope recalled. "She would claim that her guns and money had been taken, and she'd make accusations against Kenneth, saying he'd

40

stolen things from her, that he had hit her, but by the time our men arrived, Kenneth Smith would be nowhere in sight and she'd have no signs of physical abuse and no receipts or proof of property owned. There was not much we could do under the circumstances."

Indeed, Susan could not rely on the police to protect her, and nothing she owned was safe for long. When something of hers was stolen, she would blame Kenneth and his friends, but that never got her anywhere. Even her large-screen TV, rented from a Matewan furnishings place—was stolen. As usual, Susan called the West Virginia police and made allegations against Kenneth, but a few days later, things blew over.

Domestic violence was now a part of her daily life. Although Kenneth claims he never beat Susan, he admits he threatened her on several occasions. Tennis Daniels was living with the Smiths in 1986, and he witnessed some of their domestic squabbles. He even heard Kenneth say he'd tied Susan's hands together with a towel once, so he could slap her. But Tennis considered that none of his business. He lived at their house free of charge, so Kenneth seemed to be a good brother-in-law. Tennis knew the lease for the house was in Susan's name, but he was grateful to Kenneth, as the man of the house, for letting him stay there.

The attitudes of the males around her infuriated Susan, especially since she had to assume all the responsibilities and gained little respect in return. She often complained to her sister Shelby about her wretched life, but Shelby really was not in any position to help her. As time passed, Susan grew more and more resentful of Kenneth, suspecting him of stealing from her, blaming him for jeopardizing what little income she had. She was collecting welfare from both Kentucky and West Virginia agencies in order to make ends meet.

According to her sister Carla, collecting welfare from both states was commonplace for people living in the tricorner, the area being so isolated and dangerous, people from state agencies never came around to check on living arrangements. And since state borders literally run right across everyone's backyard, it was easy for inhabitants to claim dual residence.

Evidently Susan was very familiar with both systems, because she knew all the right things to say in each state when she went in to fill out her disability and welfare forms. Carla remembers her sister laughing about lying to the people behind the Social Security desk in West Virginia.

Outwardly, Susan tried not to take things very seriously. Still, it mortified her to be strapped to a man who forced her to use her children as a means of income. That may have contributed to her increasing drug use. At any rate, she didn't care about the possible effects of the drugs, but seized upon anything available to her through Kenneth and the various "quack" doctors in the area. Susan used uppers, downers, cocaine, painkillers, whatever she could get her hands on.

Nonetheless, she was usually able to function well, and the people around her never realized that she was "high" most of the time. She had reached a level where she had no sense of self-worth, nothing to live for save her children. She once told her sister Carla, "I've gotten to the point where the only thing that matters to me is my kids."

So it seemed all the worse to think that she had no one to thank but herself for the mess she was in. No amount of nail polish or facial cream or peroxide could disguise her dreadful existence.

Susan was looking for some man who'd come along and rescue her, take her out of her miserable existence. But no one in his right mind would bother with anyone from Freeburn, she told herself bitterly. And between her financial difficulties and her low self-esteem, she resigned herself to the fact that she could not get out of the trap. Certainly no outsider would ever enter the tricorner world and take her away from the people in and around the Tug, people who were always scheming.

In the meantime, Cat Eyes Lockhart got paroled in the summer of 1986, and he found temporary shelter in places not far from his Kentucky home. He was thirty-two years old with no money and no hope of employment, and he was forced to "camp out" in the back yard with his old girlfriend, Sherri Justice, who resided with her mother in Home Creek, Virginia. It was an inconvenient arrangement, the area swarming with chiggers, mosquitoes, and other summer pests much of the time. So from there, he drifted from one friend's house to another in and around the tristate corner, where Virginia, West Virginia, and Kentucky come together.

From the moment Cat Eyes got out of prison, friends say he was planning his next bank robbery. He bought himself a used Dodge Colt for five hundred dollars from G. L. Rose Enterprises in Virginia and rattled around in it, staking out the many small bank branches in the tricorner vicinity. He spent hours each day driving by the dinky brick structures, places that looked like brick homes, save for the drive-in windows and the tiny unlit bank names.

These banks were perfect targets for him, so he watched to see what times of day the managers and tellers arrived, working out his plan to hit a chain of banks all at once. With his arrest record and his successful heist in Grundy, Cat Eyes had now turned professional. He was no longer an impulsive street criminal. He was ready to take on the whole tricorner area, and had even come to view himself as a hero, every day devising ways to improve on his techniques. He was certain it wouldn't be long before he could be able to dress well again, drive around in flashy cars, and regain the respect he'd once gotten from the local criminals he called his friends.

However, in the months while Cat Eyes was planning the bank robberies, the weather grew cold, and he tired of camping outside at Home Creek, so he temporarily moved in with his mother up in Vulcan. Of course it wasn't long before he went to visit his old buddy, Kenneth, who had been living down the road with Susan and the kids for two and a half years.

Chapter Three

Born on the Fourth of July in 1959, Mark Steven Putnam was the eldest of three children raised in a rural and pleasant New England town, Conventry, Connecticut, about thirty-five miles east of Hartford. His parents, Barbara and Walter Putnam, built a house there in 1968, near the shores of Lake Wangumbaug. Walter, a truck driver for Sears, was a well-respected man in the community. Barbara was a housewife, a good mother, and a religious woman. With her two boys and her daughter, she attended St. Mary's Catholic Church each Sunday.

The Putnams were hardworking, all-American folks. They spent summer holidays at the lake or at the public beach at Patriot's Park, and celebrated special occasions at the town's inviting country-style restaurants.

Mark Putnam went to the Robertson Elementary School, located in the working-class section of town. There he made friends mostly with kids from his own lower income bracket. According to townsfolk who knew him as a boy, he was a quiet kid who did the usual things. He played sports in the park, ate at the local pizza parlor, and attended summer concerts at the nearby outdoor band shell.

But as a youth, Mark had handsome, chiseled features, and his thick long hair and alluring eyes won him praise from women of all ages. People often said he could be a model if he were just a bit taller. In seventh grade, Mark entered the Middle School, located near downtown Coventry, and was a tremendous hit with all the girls. While in junior high, he became an active athlete, playing on the baseball, basketball, and soccer teams.

His junior-high soccer and basketball coach, Peter Sturrock, said Putnam was the best athlete they had, excelling as the captain of the soccer team and co-captain of the basketball team. Sturrock had nothing but respect for his former star player.

"Mark was an overachiever, a real hard worker, kind of driven to do well—and one of the nicest kids I knew," Sturrock recalled. "He was a leader, highly competitive. In a soccer game, when Mark was goalie, he'd be yelling at his players to get them to move. Out on the sports field he was very aggressive. He had no fear of getting hurt. He'd jump at somebody's foot to stop a goal. He'd do anything to win."

However, while he came on strong and overly aggressive on the sports field, Mark seemed quite the opposite in his everyday dealings with people. Off the field, he was reclusive, very cautious in the way he approached teachers and classmates, extremely shy and private about his personal life. Many young women at school had a crush on him, and he got teased about it by fellow players and friends, but he seemed to turn off any interest in that side of his life, giving others the impression that he wasn't interested in girls.

Sturrock says some of his athletes asked him for advice in personal matters, but not Mark Putnam. Mark listened to Sturrock when the coach addressed the group, but he never sought him out.

"I was a resource to the kids in many ways. They'd ask me about forming relationships, and I would give all the kids advice," Sturrock said. "I tried to tell the kids to develop respect for all human beings. Not to get caught up in that macho thing of keeping score. We'd talk more about the girls' feelings. I told them that if you went into a relationship with integrity and honesty, then you'd never have to second-guess yourself. But I don't recall Mark ever asking me any questions about girls. He just wasn't the type of kid to talk about it."

Sturrock thought perhaps Mark's shyness stemmed from his working-class background. He said it was possible Putnam was uncomfortable with kids from more affluent families.

"I think a lot of Mark's friends were from a lower socioeconomic background, possibly on welfare, although the Putnams were not on welfare," Sturrock remembers. "Mark was very comfortable with working-class people. He grew up in a nice little house, but they didn't have a lot of things. It was very modest. The family was just hanging in there economically. They'd meet their bills."

According to Sturrock, Mark was one of the kids who got economic assistance for the purchase of athletic uniforms, though he hadn't asked for help. He'd been too proud to admit that he needed anything, and the coach had had to offer him aid.

When Putnam left junior high, he went next door to Capt. Nathan Hale High School, just like everyone else, but he stayed there for just one school year, 1974-75. He was the number one soccer player, a top all-around athlete and before the year was out, he was awarded an athletic scholarship to the exclusive Pomfret School, a prep school fifty miles from Coventry and a whole world away from Mark's home.

In addition to its reputation for providing a quality education, Pomfret offered Mark an introduction to the lifestyle of the super rich. He had entered into the world of high society, and as a star athlete in an academy that had fourteen athletic teams — including a championship crew and squash and ice hockey teams — Putnam had it made.

While there, his athletic experience revealed his commitment to hard work. His leadership on the field and his dedication to sports was looked at as a triumph for his school. At Pomfret, Mark played basketball, baseball, and soccer, becoming the soccer team's captain in his senior year when the team went undefeated and won its division championship. "Captain Putt led the way," the *Pomfret School Bulletin* often announced beneath pictures of Mark in his Number 11 soccer jersey. And he received the attention a star athlete is accorded. His father and former coaches would travel each week to cheer him on to victory; his classmates were in awe of him; at home, the whole town was proud of the local boy who "made good."

Still, Putnam must have felt out of place in such posh surroundings. He was there, after all, not because his family could afford to send him, but because he'd received an athletic scholarship. Since that did not cover the cost of room and board, he was one of the school's "commuter" students, traveling back and forth from Coventry each day in a car pool. Mark often rode with his good friend, Mike Rodensky. The two of them are pictured together in his senior yearbook sitting atop an Oldsmobile, Mark in a crew-neck sweater, corduroy slacks, and Topsider shoes, looking very much the prep-school kid. He graduated from the preparatory school in the class of 1978, leaving with a strong sense of purpose and the drive to use his abilities to their limits.

Mark went on to the University of Tampa, where he majored in criminology. He made the dean's list in his first year, and as was anticipated, he excelled in sports, becoming captain of Tampa's NCAA champion soccer team in his senior year. In fact, in his last two years at UT, the Spartan soccer team enjoyed its best seasons in the team's history. With Putnam playing defense, the team went undefeated, winning the NCAA Division II championship at Yale University in 1982. It was a dream come true for Putnam, returning to Connecticut and beating the team of the Ivy League institution he had revered his whole life. Nathan Hale had been a Yale graduate, so Mark had grown up in awe of the place. Finally he triumphed there, winning praises from everyone around him.

At Tampa, Putnam wasn't the typical "jock" who made it with the ladies by throwing his weight around. He was a hard worker, tough on the field; but he remained shockingly quiet about his personal life. No one really heard Putnam brag about conquests or the number of young women he went out with. According to some of his teammates, Mark seemed to exhibit the same qualities his coaches and teachers had noticed years before — aggression in sports and in class but extreme caution about divulging information about his private affairs.

"Putnam was an overachiever, easily the best student on the team," said his teammate Kenny James. "Mark was an incredibly intense player," another teammate, Jim Foytlk, recalled, "but off the field, he was almost shy — not glamorous at all." His soccer coach at Tampa, Jay Miller, said Mark was a silent leader, one who led by example.

"We'd do running through the downtown streets of Tampa at seven A.M. every morning and he'd always win the three-mile race," Miller said. The standard thing was how close the next guy could get to Putnam; he was so far ahead of everybody. One time, a teammate got real close to him, so Mark sprinted the rest of the way. He just had to be number one. That was his nature."

Miller said Putnam was a good team captain, respected by all, and he gave one hundred percent to his team. When Putnam dislocated his arm in a game during his junior year, he still insisted on playing, the coach added. "And a lot of times a trainer would go out on the field and pop his arm back in. Then Mark would just go on with the game — he was determined."

Always well-liked in college, Mark was apparently an all-around nice guy who, by that time, got along well with people from all walks of life and had no trouble fitting in with any group. When it came to women, Miller noted that Mark had plenty, but apparently there was no particular pattern to his taste in girlfriends. Although Mark had come to Tampa from an expensive private high school, that world hadn't spoiled him. He wasn't particularly interested in girls with money or girls who were glamorous. As his coach recalls, Mark's dates came from all different social levels.

"He dated just like everyone else. He always had a girlfriend. Over a four-year period, there were four girlfriends. Some would hang around the soccer team after a game, and from what I could see, there wasn't any particular type he seemed to stick with. Each girl was different," Miller said. "None of his former girlfriends had ill feelings for him, because he never jilted them. He was sensitive; that was Mark. But he was a good-looking guy, so he was tough for women to keep hold of."

While in college, Mark told his soccer coach that his big dream was to be an FBI agent. Majoring in criminology with a 3.0 grade-point average, he was taking courses such as Criminal Investigation, which covered crime-scene search and recording, and Deviant Behavior, which dealt with sexual perversions and violent disorders. And his college career was going smoothly. Mark was making good grades and was becoming popular with both students and teachers.

He did not now have a scholarship to help pay the cost of his education, but his family assisted him and he earned money doing odd jobs around Tampa. Initially, everything was going well for Mark. He was delighted to be in Florida, surrounded by palm trees and bikini-clad girls. It was a whole new experience, a much freer and laid-back existence than the life he had known in the staunch New England surroundings of his youth.

But when he entered his sophomore year, tragedy struck the Putnam household and Mark found himself being called back to Connecticut on a regular basis. His father, Walter, was afflicted with an incurable cancer. By the spring of his sophomore year, Mark left school for two weeks, returning to New England where he watched his father die under the strain of radiation treatments and heavy drug therapy. It was a degrading type of death which hit Mark very hard. According to others, he wasn't the type of kid who could accept his father's destruction, yet there was nothing he could do to help him.

Bruce Johnson, a family friend and pastor of the First Congregational Church of Coventry, helped the Putnams throughout the difficult period of Walter's long and drawn out death, which devastated the entire Putnam family. Johnson saw the Putnams as a close-knit group, faithful to Walter. He said they stayed at his beside in the hospital in Norwich, watching Walter struggle for months.

"It was a type of cancer that required a lot of radiation treatments, but the family was there with Walter the whole time," Johnson said. "Mark was close to his father. It was difficult for him to see his dad defeated that way. He would return from Florida during his father's periods of treatment, as I recall. Then, when death was near, he remained at his father's side."

Bruce Johnson performed the funeral for Walter Putnam on March 18, 1980. Mark was twenty. His younger brother, Tim, was just seventeen. Years later Johnson would perform

Tim Putnam's marriage ceremony and would baptize Tim's child, but he never saw much of Mark after Walter's death. Still attending college in Florida, Mark returned to Coventry every summer, but he remained a shy, quiet, reserved young man, who apparently did not open up much to anyone in that community; Bruce Johnson was no exception.

In August 1982, three months after Mark Putnam graduated from the University of Tampa, he landed a job as clerk at the FBI office in New Haven, Connecticut, the FBI headquarters for the state. Situated on the fifth floor of the Robert N. Giaimo Federal Building, an imposing, all-white edifice with revolving doors, guarded by heavy security and closed circuit cameras, the FBI office required visitors to get official clearance and to wear plastic badges upon entering. A large picture of J. Edgar Hoover, director of the FBI from 1924-1972, occupied a prominent place in the reception area. The New Haven office had between forty and fifty employees.

While working there, Putnam wasn't much noticed by the FBI agents or others higher up in the bureau. He operated the telephone switchboard, working night shifts and weekends from four P.M. to midnight or from midnight to eight A.M. He never exchanged more than casual greetings with his superiors.

But Putnam was biding his time, learning about the FBI through osmosis. It was his way of educating himself in the tricks of the trade.

An anonymous co-worker said Mark was conscientious. "He started work early — and stayed late. He was a good person to be around. He was always pleasant, polite, a real gentleman." Surely, Putnam put the extra time in because he expected it to pay off later. He had already made it clear to friends and family that he wanted to be an agent, to be in law enforcement.

Along the way, Mark Putnam had married a dark-haired beauty named Kathleen, the daughter of a man in real-estate who lived in the Manchester, Connecticut area. The two met just after he began his job at the FBI's New Haven office, Mark leaving work a bit early one fateful night to go meet Kathy upon his mother's insistence. Reportedly, Mark received a phone call from his mother, Barbara, who was out listening to some music at a local bar:

"I just met this girl, Mark," she said emphatically, "I think you better get down here."

Barbara and Kathy spent over an hour together in the bar that evening waiting for Mark's arrival. During their initial conversation, the two women evidently got pretty close and had a heart to heart talk, Kathy telling Barbara about what kind of wife she planned to be and what a wonderful mother she would make. The two women quickly became close and at some point in their conversation, before Mark arrived, Kathy turned to Barbara and said, "I've always wanted to be a mother. I want to bake cookies and play with the kids."

Barbara Putnam decided that Kathy was just the girl Mark needed. She wanted to see her son settle down, and Kathy was beautiful, with rich brown hair that made her hazel eyes jump out like stars. Moreoever, she was elegant, with tiny features, an up-turned nose, and perfectly tweezed eyebrows. And she wore very little makeup. A natural beauty.

Perhaps it was love at first sight. Perhaps Mark knew that Kathleen was the person he had been searching for. Certainly she felt that way about him, later telling a reporter he was charismatic, "the kind of guy who just melted you." At any rate, after a few hours of chitchat, Mark was already telling Kathy his life's ambitions. "He told me he wanted just two things," she later revealed. "He wanted a family, and he wanted his kids to be able to say my father's an FBI agent."

Just two years younger than Mark, Kathy was the residential manager of a luxury apartment complex, and she was studying to be a paralegal. She believed in long-lasting love. Her parents were sound people. "We fit perfectly," Kathy later recalled, and she admitted that the two of them had spent that night together.

For the next two years, Kathy and Mark lived together in her luxurious Connecticut apartment. They didn't socialize much. They were both loners. On weekends, they'd go to New York City for a romantic dinner and would sometimes get tickets to a Broadway show. In the summer, they'd often hit the beaches in

Rhode Island. They loved each other, and they planned to achieve their dream: two kids, a house in Florida, and Mark's becoming an FBI agent.

In 1984, they were married on Easter weekend by a justice of the peace in New York City. However, neighbors in Pikeville remember seeing elaborate wedding pictures of Mark and Kathy, so presumably the couple had a formal wedding celebration at some point, complete with bridesmaids, floral bouquets, and a wedding cake.

Kathy became pregnant very soon after they were wed and gave birth to their daughter, Danielle, at a nearby hospital in Hartford. She quit her position as a resident manager and went to work for an insurance company, leaving that job after a short time. Kathy was not a career woman; she wanted to be a "career mom," as she repeatedly told family and friends.

Meanwhile, Putnam continued to do good work during his stint at the FBI's New Haven office, and in January of 1986, when he qualified to take the entrance exam for the FBI Academy in Quantico, Virginia, Putnam left the New Haven office. Reportedly, going from a clerical position to being a special agent is rare, but Putnam was determined to beat the odds. After applying to the Bureau, the IRS, and several police academies, and after a brief stint with Burns International Security in Hartford, Putnam was accepted into the Connecticut Police Academy, but was ousted after just nine days because of an arm injury suffered during his soccer career. Then, in mid 1986, Mark Putnam received word that he had been appointed to the FBI Academy. He was finally on his way to becoming a full-fledged FBI agent.

While Putnam awaited notification to report for the FBI training course in Quantico, he returned to work at the FBI's New Haven office, in a better job than he had formerly held, and he was also working at a liquor store, trying to build a nest egg for his young family. By the time he was to arrive for training at the FBI Academy, he wanted to be financially ready to make that move.

The FBI Academy is located on the Marine Corps base in Quantico, just fifty miles southwest of Washington, D.C., where the surroundings are heavily wooded. The facility is somewhat similar to a small college, with regular classroom buildings and dormitories. When newly appointed Special Agents report to the FBI Academy, they take an oath and then undergo training for approximately sixteen weeks — classroom instruction, physical fitness testing, and firearms training. While in training, they receive a regular salary.

Agent trainees must demonstrate proficiency in firearms, mastery of defensive tactics, and expertise in simulated arrest situations, which are carried out at the FBI's notorious Hogan's Alley, a re-created street, not unlike a Hollywood set. They must also pass two examinations, including one on FBI conduct, rules, and regulations. Special Agent applicants must also undergo a formal interview, a urinalysis for drug use, and a polygraph examination at some point during or prior to their training period.

As would be expected, the regimen at the FBI Academy is grueling. The days begin early, and training sometimes lasts well into the night. It is mentally and physically strenuous. Trainees must do pull-ups, push-ups, sit-ups, and they must score highly on a one hundred twenty-yard shuttle run and on a two-mile run. They are told that as FBI agents they will be required to relocate and to serve a one-year probationary period under the guidance of a veteran Special Agent.

During his training, Mark Putnam learned that being an FBI agent was not a "nine to five" career. He would be required to work nights, weekends, and holidays. Moreover, the work would be very demanding: he would be required to carry a weapon; he might be called upon to use deadly force to protect lives; and he would be involved in every phase of investigative work, including surveillance, interviewing witnesses and suspects, apprehending fugitives and criminals, collecting evidence, and providing testimony in court.

In addition, Putnam learned that once he had the credentials of an FBI Special Agent, his training in firearms and defensive tactics would not end. Along with the rest of the ten thousand

FBI agents operating out of field offices, he would be required to undergo routine firearms training at least four times a year, to do additional work in defensive hand-to-hand combat, to attend two to three sessions in which he would be brought up to date on federal law and recent supreme court decisions.

Mark Putnam graduated from the Academy on October 6, 1986, and was issued his gold FBI badge in the shape of a shield. He was now officially a part of the investigative arm of the US Department of Justice. His dream had come true.

In February of 1987, Special Agent Putnam got his first FBI assignment, to the isolated two-man office in Pikeville, Kentucky. In Pikeville, Putnam would operate under the tutelage of Special Agent Dan Brennan. He would learn how to work in the field, handle informants, and live with danger. His duties would include investigations into public corruption, bank robberies, interstate criminal activity, the apprehension of fugitives, and drug-trafficking matters. Putnam felt challenged.

But Kathy Putnam didn't like the sound of Pikeville and didn't want to move there. Mark had originally been assigned to the Louisville office, and Kathy had even gone down there with her dad to look at housing. Then word had come that Pikeville, not Louisville, would be Mark's assignment.

"Usually," Kathy later told reporters, "new agents are assigned to a big office." And she had been sure Mark could be reassigned to the original Louisville location. According to one reporter, Kathy viewed herself as the force in the marriage. She saw herself as the one with the brains and the money, and she felt she was running things from behind the scenes. However, she couldn't win on this one. Mark wouldn't refuse the Pikeville post. He told her he looked at it as an opportunity. But Kathy believed it was just that nobody else would go there. She saw Pikeville as the worst possible assignment, a place out in the middle of nowhere, two and a half hours away from the nearest airport.

Allegedly, Kathy phoned the FBI's D.C. headquarters, insisting that Putnam wasn't suited for the Pikeville assignment. He was too inexperienced, she told them. He belonged in a large office, not a two-man one. When an FBI official responded that Putnam was the best candidate for the challenging position in Pikeville because of his prior police experience, Kathy reminded him that her husband had merely been a police trainee, never a member of the Connecticut force, but her pleas fell on deaf ears.

Like it or not, the Putnams were on their way to Pikeville. Mark moved there first, purchasing a seven-room house for one hundred and fifty thousand dollars on the "pleasant" side of town. Kathy would follow a couple of months later, having stayed behind to take care of any loose ends in Connecticut.

Chapter Four

Pikeville, a fourth-class city and the seat of the Pike County, is located on US 23/460, one hundred seventy-two miles southeast of downtown Louisville. Originally called Piketon at its inception in 1825, it was named for Zebulon Pike, a U.S. Army explorer and discoverer of Pike's Peak. The city is about nine miles long and half a mile wide. It runs through the mountains in the shape of a horseshoe and is, surprisingly, Kentucky's third largest banking center. Unlike many eastern Kentucky mountain towns, Pikeville has a busy downtown filled with professional offices, a fair share of greasy-spoon restaurants, furniture and clothing stores, and crowded streets.

As the county seat, it plays host to many of the county's estimated seventy-nine thousand residents during the work week, especially on the first of the month, when welfare checks arrive in the mail. On that day, city people see country folk coming down from the "hollers" in beat-up old vehicles with carloads of barefoot children. Pikevillians just shake their heads in anger and disgust, hateful of the "hillbilly" stereotype these people perpetuate. Pikevillians don't understand why the hill people can't become more civilized, why they can't get jobs and work their way out of crippling poverty.

Most of the folks out in Pike county don't have adequate housing and can't afford decent clothes. They live in trailers stuck up against hillsides, and they walk around in clothes purchased second or third hand. At last count, there were eleven thousand mobile homes registered in Pike County. These are a luxury to many of the local folks, those who have to make do in old shacks made of plywood.

However, tucked away amid the poverty-ridden masses are a large number of coal-rich millionaires. Inside the Pikeville city limits, or within a ten-mile radius of town, live more than a hundred people with a net worth of a million dollars or more, making this area one of those with the largest concentration of millionaires in Kentucky. Many of these coal magnates are not snobs, although a handful do view themselves as rulers of a little kingdom while turning their backs on their neighbor's problems and living in mansions.

Some of the wealthy wear overpriced, flashy jewelry and clothing, and often boast of having met the likes of President George Bush and the First Lady at high-priced political fund raisers.

A number have had their pictures taken with more than one United States President, and they proudly display these photos in their offices and homes.

The disparity between rich and poor probably contributes to the local crime problem, the news being cluttered with reports of bank robberies, lootings, and slayings; of stories about men knifing each other in parking lots, drug dealers having shootouts, and people using Uzi machine guns and other assault weapons to enforce their own brand of mountain justice.

When Mark Putnam arrived in town to work with Daniel Brennan, the Special Agent in charge of Pikeville, allegedly he discovered that the area's backwardness had filtered over into the FBI office. Brennan had been a special agent for fourteen years and was nearing retirement age. Rumor had it that he was more interested in his boat than in crime. Putnam learned this in the first few days on this assignment, and he soon realized he would have to handle more work than he thought tolerable.

Before Kathy arrived, Mark informed her in their telephone conversations that he was carrying much of the weight at the tiny outpost. He said he wasn't sure he was ready to handle an office where he'd have such a heavy burden. It has been reported that he was scared, and fellow law enforcement workers believed Putnam was suffering from culture shock.

It must have been a great relief for him when Kathy arrived with Danielle in April of 1987.

His wife seemed happy to be with him, and she liked the nearly new seven-room house they purchased in a subdivision called Cedar Gap. It was a charming place, just outside town and right around the corner from Special Agent Dan Brennan's handsome brick house.

Modern, the Putnams' home had large rooms and good-sized picture windows, a front porch with a wicker swing, pink azalea bushes in the yard, and a two-car garage. Their neighbors were college professors, lawyers, doctors; well-to-do professionals who had two or three cars in their driveways — BMWs, Mercedes, Range Rovers. Compared to the other houses on the street, the Putnams' place was somewhat modest. It wasn't elaborately landscaped and had no ornate gates.

Mark began to like the Pikeville area. Despite the poverty around him, the people in Cedar Gap were affluent, and he decided the post wasn't so bad after all. Being a joiner and born leader, Mark did all he could to befriend his neighbors, to aid the local police forces, and to "fit in" with the Southern way of life.

But Kathy did not like her new environment. She felt she had nothing in common with anyone around her. The local twang got on her nerves, as did the greasy cooking and the beauty shops operating out of trailers. As far as Kathy was concerned, she had been sentenced to two years in exile; nevertheless, she resolved to make the best of it, at least for a while.

"Mark had the job he wanted, and I loved our

house," she later told reporters. "We were talking about how good this could be, because in a small office in a place like Pikeville, with everything that was going on, he could really make a name for himself."

However, not long after Kathy settled in, the Putnams started spending little time together. Mark's work kept him busy nights and weekends. He often worked twelve or fourteen hours straight. Determined to earn a name for himself in the community, he also spent many of his off hours away from home. He coached soccer at the local YMCA. He attended the St. Francis Catholic Church regularly — by himself. On Friday nights, he attended the Pikeville High School football games, going out for drinks with friends afterward. The local people liked him, which was, he told Kathy, crucial to his job. He had to befriend everybody in order to get the inside scoop on crime in the area.

Unfortunately, things were not going as well for Kathy. Now well along in her pregnancy with their second child, she was becoming increasingly irritated by her lonely existence. Unhappy most of the time, she paced the floors inside her home, attached to her parents and her Connecticut lifestyle only by telephone. To her, there were no decent restaurants in the area, no suitable movies ever were shown in town, and Pikeville had no satisfactory stores. With no theater, no museums, and no concerts, Kathy felt like a captive at the ends of the Earth. She would later say that Pikeville was like a wasteland.

"There was nothing there for me. The grocery store and the K Mart. That was it," she complained. "I was used to civilization. You couldn't even get in your car to drive. It was only a matter of time before you were caught in the mountains — and I was scared to death to drive in them."

Worst of all for Kathy was the small-town mentality of the locals, the idea that everybody knew who she was and wanted to know what she was doing. On her third day in town, she said she went to the bank and the teller looked up and exclaimed, "Oh, you must be the FBI's wife. How do you like your house on Honeysuckle?"

It was that kind of intrusion that Kathy disliked. She was a private person. That was why she and Mark had gotten along so well. She didn't want people talking about her finances or poking their noses into her personal affairs.

She and Mark had kept to themselves ever since they'd met in 1982. They both shied away from gossip. Now, suddenly, she had neighbors who looked out their windows and sat on their porches, seemingly watching her every move. It was unbearable. She couldn't believe these people had nothing better to do than wonder what was going on inside her home, inside her bedroom, inside her head. Their intrusiveness infuriated her.

Once, when Mark had been gone all night, meeting with his supervisor in Louisville, a neighbor knocked on the door the next morning and said, "I couldn't help noticing that Mark's car wasn't in the driveway last night." To Kathy, Pikeville was a fishbowl. Its residents ogled her, minded her business, and made up tales about her.

The local gossip and inquisitiveness of her neighbors only caused Kathy to become more and more withdrawn, and for the most part, she declined to talk to anyone except Mark and Danielle. For a while, she busied herself with her elaborate dollhouse creations, building wonderful lilliputian structures complete with tiny furnishings, which she took to the local strip malls for "showings." But as the months went on and people continually seemed overly interested in Kathy's personal life, she gave up her dollhouse hobby and refused to associate with anyone in the town.

It got to the point where she balked at picking Danielle up from the day-care center in which Mark had enrolled her. Not wanting to deal with the people there, she had Mark retrieve their daughter from the Model Daycare Center.

Danielle attended the center because Kathy ran back to Connecticut whenever she could. She often took Danielle with her, but because Mark missed his daughter, this day care became a necessity.

Of course, the people around her thought Kathy Putnam was unusual, and one of her neighbors, Mrs. Kathy Sohn, talked about Kathy Putnam's peculiar behavior:

"I tried to reach out to her, you know. I brought a cake over there when they moved in. I did all the usual stuff. I invited them for dinner, but only Mark came over to eat. She never came to my home. Sometimes I would drop in on her, but she was always to herself. She was unhappy. That was apparent. The only thing she talked about was what she was preparing for Mark's dinner. She'd be cooking some kind of meat and potatoes, just typical dishes, nothing gourmet, and she'd say she was getting the food ready for Mark just in case he came home early."

According to Mrs. Sohn, the only time she was able to get any insight into Kathy Putnam was when she met her parents in 1987, during the Putnams' first year in Pikeville. She said it was the only visit Mark Putnam's in-laws made, and she recalled that Kathy seemed unusually friendly and perky while her parents were there. She had even talked about her dad helping her with some projects around the house, things Mark didn't have time for, and she asked about painting the trim in the same dark gray color the Sohns had used. In the two years the Sohns and Putnams were neighbors, that was the only substantive conversation Mrs. Sohn ever had with Kathy.

Outside of Kathy's parents, no out-of-town visitors came to the Putnams' home, and because they had no mutual friends in Pikeville, and had not joined any of the local organizations or charity groups, they were isolated, locked away in the secrecy of their home. Even their daughter had few friends. It seems her mother did not encourage her to play with the neighborhood children.

Laura, the Sohns' twelve-year-old daughter, went over to play with Danielle a number of times because she felt sorry for the lonely little three-year-old. Allegedly Kathy Putnam didn't let Danielle out-of-doors much, so the child spent a great deal of time in her playroom. Whenever Laura came by for a brief visit, Danielle's face would light up. Laura remembers Kathy as being distant and disinterested in her daughter's playthings, and she recalls that Kathy was usually on the phone, talking to some member of her family or to a friend in Connecticut.

"Kathy was real quiet, she would never say much to me," Laura said. "She wore black a lot, and she never went outside. It was strange. I never got to know her — I never even knew she was pregnant. Sometimes I would go over there with Dan Brennan's daughter, Katie. The two of us would go and play with Danielle because she was hardly let outside. She was always happy to see us."

Laura remembers Danielle's play room, filled with every conceivable expensive toy which Danielle said her grandparents had bought her. Danielle would take out her newest Fisher-Price toy, or would show Laura the Putnam family photo albums, pictures of her parents' wedding, pictures of her family trip to

Disneyworld, things like that. Like most three year olds, Danielle liked to spend time musing over the photo albums, talking about her trips to Connecticut, or Florida. She would point to herself in these shots. From what Laura could gather, the photos indicated that Kathy's parents owned a home in Connecticut and another in Florida. She got the impression that they were well set financially.

Mark, meanwhile, was gone from home often. When he wasn't working, he went out with some of his acquaintances in town. He drank beer at the Boulevard, the local dance club where many of the patrons knew he was an FBI agent, of course never during working hours. After a football game or on a Saturday evening he'd drop into the club, however. Apparently he no longer worried about obliging Kathy.

While he couldn't seem to get his wife to go out, Danielle was delighted to go on "dates" with him. Every Friday night, he and his daughter would get dressed up, even before a football game, and he would take her out to Coal Run Village, about seven miles away, where they would eat at a McDonald's or Dairy Queen, then visit the pet store at the strip shopping center. It would always be just the two of them. Mark carried a picture of Danielle at all times, and would brag about his daughter to his fellow law enforcement workers, often telling local policemen how bright and delicate she was. It was a way to pass the time during the tedious hours spent on stakeouts.

In December of 1987, exactly nine months after Kathy moved to Pikeville, Mark, Jr., was born. Kathy went to Connecticut to give birth to the baby, staying with her parents for almost three months after the delivery. She refused to give birth in Pikeville. She had paid one visit to the local OBGYN, Dr. Harry Altman, and had been infuriated by the long time she'd spent in his waiting room. Used to preferential treatment, she couldn't stand the idea that only one doctor serviced so many women, she off-handedly told Kathy Sohn.

During her absence, Mark got some extra days off from work in order to spend a few weekends with her, and at Christmas time, he took two weeks off to be with his young family in Connecticut, asking the Sohns to keep an eye on the house. Back in Pikeville, everyone thought he and Kathy were the perfect couple, well suited in looks and demeanor. Mark seemed a concerned and loving daddy and husband, Kathy a doting housewife who cooked from scratch and created a happy home. When little Mark took his first baby steps, Kathy called the state police and had them patch her through to Mark's radio. When he got the patched-in call, he sped to her side, using his siren, Code 2.

Lee Deramus, who worked at Pikeville's Model Daycare Center, had nothing but compliments for the whole family. She looked up to Putnam and was especially fond of his pretty little daughter.

"Danielle was very smart, a sweet child — very well adjusted. And Kathy was gorgeous. She had long dark hair. She was thin. She was classy and she dressed like a lady, although I never saw her much. Mark was the one who usually picked Danielle up," Deramus recalled. "We called him the gorgeous FBI agent, you know, whenever he would come in to see what Danielle had been doing that day, what pictures she drew, and things like that. I thought he and his wife were a beautiful couple. Mark was always loving and caring. He had a smile on his face anytime you'd talk to him, and his daughter was that way, always loving and happy. You could see that she and her daddy loved each other."

However, not everyone saw Mark as a loving father. His neighbor, Sohn, a psychology professor at Pikeville College, remembers a different Putnam. He can still visualize him driving to and from work every day, always keeping his eyes fixed on the road straight ahead. The Putnams each had a sedan-type vehicle: Mark's was brown; Kathy's was blue. And in a region filled with coal dust and dirty cars, Sohn recalls that Putnam's immaculate brown car stood out. It was an unmarked four-door Dodge Diplomat, fully equipped with all the latest in hidden policy technology, and Putnam bragged about the car to Sohn, proud that the vehicle had been provided him compliments of the FBI. Sohn saw Mark as a kid striving to fit into a man's boots.

"Whenever Mark passed my house, I would

think he always looked much older than he was. He always looked serious, and he slouched forward over the steering wheel a bit," Sohn remembered. "I thought the view of him in this 'old man's' car was in sharp contrast to his youthful body and spirit. He always looked very proper and disciplined, but he was only in his twenties."

According to Sohn, Mark was around the neighborhood often enough, but he seemed to leave home earlier and return later than most of the men on the street. Of course Sohn thought that was not unusual for a man in law enforcement. What he did find unusual was that the Putnams had very little furniture in their home. It seemed they didn't plan to stay there long.

In Sohn's estimation, Mark and Kathy Putnam had moved into a "manufactured" house, a two-story structure built very quickly, without much attention paid to detail or quality. Putnam brightened the place up with shrubbery and painted it a light gray, giving it a sophisticated look; however, inside the house, there was nothing to indicate a happy, well-adjusted lifestyle. There were no pictures on the walls, there were no collections of objects or books, no conversation pieces. The place was very stark, Sohn had noticed, much the way Putnam appeared to be when he was on his way to work, always wearing a starched white shirt and a sports coat. His coat barely covered his pistol. He was an all work and no play kind of guy when he was on the job, Sohn thought, the picture-perfect FBI man.

Sohn knew Putnam was an athlete, and the two young men occasionally went jogging together at the town track just minutes away from their street. Sohn recalls watching Putnam jog six or eight miles, sometimes taking off full tilt up a mile-long hill, then doing a set of very fast chin-ups, and finally running four-forties around the track. And whenever Putnam ran, he wore skimpy shorts and a tight shirt, showing off his muscular body.

At times Sohn thought Putnam a bit of a show-off, but he also knew him in a different light—as a fellow worshiper at Pikeville's St. Francis Catholic Church. Still, Sohn never got close to Putnam, not even in the setting of the church, because Putnam always sat alone in the same pew, and did not stay after the service for the customary coffee-and-doughnuts social hour.

"I can see him kneeling in the center of the church, just to the right of the center of the pew. He wore a white shirt, open at the neck, no tie. You always knew his gun was under his coat. You just knew cause he kind of talked about it. It was important to him, that he was an agent," Sohn said. "Father Hopinjohns, our priest, went to visit the Putnams at their home on many occasions. Father Hop went over there because he felt sorry for Kathy. He knew she was very lonely."

On warm evenings, the people on Honeysuckle Drive would usually stand out on the street, watching their children play as they held friendly conversations. Sohn recalls the Putnams wore mostly shorts and white T-shirts with tennis shoes or flip-flops around the neighborhood. He was a laid-back guy who would stroll down the street with Danielle in a baby carriage. He became very much a part of the neighborhood scene.

But he also remembers that any time he talked with Putnam the conversation usually turned into a discussion about police work. It seems Putnam was forever boasting about his cases and the various leads he was following. He'd give Sohn all kinds of information regarding his FBI work, and that seemed strange to Sohn. "Shouldn't FBI business be kept confidential?" he asked.

"I can remember in the 1988 Presidential campaign, Jesse Jackson was pushing his drug platform, and Putnam told me he was trying to develop a drug case in eastern Kentucky. He even named local sheriff's deputies he said were a part of the problem. Putnam claimed he could get no help, no cooperation from them in solving the drug problem, because they were involved in it," Sohn recollected. When he named names I thought the whole discussion a bit risky, but I listened because I figured any drug trafficking in town might someday affect my kids. I was concerned."

Not that Putnam was a one-sided individual, all police talk. He was still a great athlete, and he wanted to be recognized as such. Mark coached the Sohns' son in soccer, along with dozens of other kids, winning a lot of friends in the community; and eventually most people trusted and liked him. When the Sohns went way to Arizona for several months, Mark Putnam watched their house. They believed him to be honest and caring, and could think of no one better to trust with their key.

"Putnam wanted to help out. He wanted to be the big guy. He wanted to watch our house while we were gone, like a big protector," Sohn said. "Funny thing was, when we returned he never gave our key back—he was too preoccupied—and then he moved without ever bothering to say goodbye. It was like he wanted to just forget all about us."

In any case, it was the general perception that Mark Putnam was a man who wanted people's respect, and he seemed to try to earn it by discussing his cases—the bank robberies, the stolen heavy equipment, the drug corruption. He liked people to think of him as a tough policy type.

And much to Putnam's pleasure, from the moment he arrived in Pikeville, he had plenty of opportunities to fill the "big law enforcement" shoes. The area had recently been hit with a rash of bank robberies, and both Kentucky and West Virginia State Police had a number of leads and were in hot pursuit of the perpetrators. A lot of important investigative work had to be done by Putnam and his partner, Dan Brennan, because there seemed to be a pattern, which led police to believe that one robber was responsible for the majority of the robberies. The banks, located on both sides of the Kentucky and West Virginia state line, were all robbed in a similar fashion: the criminals used sawed-off shotguns, hid their identities by wearing ski masks, and escaped in stolen vehicles.

If Putnam could solve the bank-robbery problem, he thought he might land himself a transfer to an FBI office in some desirable location, one where he and Kathy could live happily together and raise their two kids in peace and harmony.

Susan Smith, by early 1987, was pacing around her house and asking herself, "What have I done?" she wondered why she had hitched herself to a guy her family considered a certifiable creep. She had stayed with Kenneth all these years and had been so unhappy. He played around. He beat her. He stole from her. Why didn't she leave him, just take off? Did she lack guts?

But every time she questioned why she remained, she always came up with a defense for Kenneth, a way to make him seem all right. She would convince herself that he would change, that her family was too critical of him; would tell herself that he really wasn't all bad, that he loved the children more than anything. And he was a good daddy, always bringing them home gifts and spending a lot of time with them. Brady and Miranda truly loved him. They looked up to their daddy.

But whenever Kenneth hit her or abused her verbally, Susan would go running to her sister, Shelby, for comfort, screaming about wanting out of the relationship.

"Why don't you just throw that bum out of there?" Shelby would say.

"I know I should. I keep telling him if he doesn't leave I will," Susan would answer.

"But why the hell should you be the one to go? It's your goddamn house, Suzie, not his! Now why don't you just kick him the hell out!"

"But then what do I do about the kids? No, I'd have to be the one to leave, and then there's Tennis in the guest room. Where would he go?"

"Why should you care about Tennis? He's a grown man. Let him find his own place to live at. You don't need to be feeding him and all those damn tramps he brings around. You've got to look out for your own self."

But Susan never took Shelby's advice. Instead she went on taking care of her children, her brother, her ex-husband, and any of his friends who might happen to need shelter or a meal. And whatever house repairs needed to be done, she did herself. If the gutters needed to be cleared, it was Susan who climbed to empty them. If a room needed painting, she bought tarps and brushes and handled the job, possibly with the help of another brother, Billy Joe. As far as household chores went, Susan did all of them.

So in June of 1987, when Cat Eyes came around asking to stay with Kenneth and Susan, offering to do odd jobs around the house in exchange for rent, Susan was happy to have him. She and Kenneth talked it over, and they were both in favor of the idea. Besides, Susan thought, having Cat Eyes there would curtail Kenneth's downright nasty behavior and might keep him out of her hair. Plus, with Cat Eyes around, Kenneth wouldn't have as much spare room for his other stray friends who appeared unannounced and uninvited every weekend.

Domestic life was just a cheap and convenient base of operation for drug-taking sessions and card games. Kenneth didn't like to be controlled or regimented, but in Cat Eyes' presence, perhaps he would be on "good behavior."

So Cat Eyes lived with the Smiths for about four months, during which time he brought his girlfriend, Sherri Justice, to stay with him. Susan didn't really know Sherri, but Cat Eyes had said she was having "problems" back in Virginia, so Susan agreed to let her stay with them at Vulcan in exchange for Sherri's help with some of the household chores. Cat Eyes didn't have any money at the time, but Susan didn't really fret about that. She was always the kind of person who, if she had a piece of bread and you were hungry, would give you half of it. Susan never asked Cat Eyes for rent money, not even after it became clear that he had plenty of cash rolling in. She did, however, make sure that

Cat Eyes supplied her with drugs.

Cat Eyes and Sherri stayed in the guest bedroom, located behind the kitchen at the back of the house. He kept his clothing in a green duffle bag, and in another bag, actually a pillowcase, he kept his guns and ski masks. He had two shotguns. One was a single barrel; the other was a double barrel, sawed-off. Cat Eyes was using the guns to pull off bank robberies, Susan was sure, but she had no proof.

He would appear one day with a wad of money, then he'd take off for a week. Then he'd reappear with a different car, then he'd be gone for ten days. There was just no keeping track of him. And Cat Eyes was sly enough not to brag about his criminal activities. He just let the rewards speak for themselves.

Meanwhile, Susan's house was busier than ever, with her brother, Tennis, now using the living-room sofa as a bed, and her brother, Billy Joe, also hanging around using Cat Eyes' room whenever Cat wasn't around. Between the kids and the assorted live-ins, it was very hectic, but Susan didn't complain. In fact, she liked all the activity, the different faces.

As a general rule, Tennis would bring home a new woman every weekend, and that in itself made life interesting. Being a handsome man, Tennis usually picked up flashy and attractive women, the type Susan liked. And her younger brother Billy Joe also brought around a few girlfriends. Susan made friends with these people and they all wound up purchasing drugs from her.

Meanwhile she maintained close contact with her family. Not a week went by that her parents didn't stop by to see her, and her three sisters, all now married with children, also visited her frequently, spending countless hours talking about the trials and tribulations of domestic life over a cup of coffee.

Unfortunately, nobody really noticed the dark side of Susan's life. They watched her take care of her children, cook their meals, and make do without much money; and everyone believed that she was managing just fine. No one knew the extent of her pent-up frustrations, or that she looked at her marriage as a failure, staying with Kenneth only because there was no one else to take his place.

As the children outgrew clothes and shoes, Susan began to feel the financial crunch more, and she started selling drugs more heavily, finding ways to hide whatever money she could from Kenneth. She became increasingly upset about being solely responsible for the children, while Kenneth just took any money brought in and gambled it away. She had, by mid 1987, lost all hope that Kenneth would change from being an uncaring, manipulative man into a loving husband and dutiful father.

Meanwhile, unbeknownst to Susan, she was under Mark Putnam's surveillance. Her house was being carefully watched by the FBI and the West Virginia State Police as well as Pike County law enforcement. Pike County Deputy

Burt Hatfield had reason to believe that Cat Eyes was the person responsible for the rash of recent bank robberies and that he was operating out of the Smith residence. He told Putnam, and the two of them routinely climbed the mountain above Susan's house, peering down at her daily activities, trying to catch a glimpse of Cat Eyes. Eventually, Hatfield decided to arrange a meeting between Putnam and the Smiths to see if they might cooperate with the FBI.

Chapter Five

"We were having a series of bank robberies, maybe one every couple of weeks. There were five banks hit about the time I called Putnam, and Mark being fresh out of the academy and all, he just jumped on it," Deputy Burt Hatfield recalls. "He was real eager to work, real energetic. When he first came out he didn't have a car, so we were pretty much taking my car everywhere. We stayed together day and night. We teamed up because I had information that was taking me into Virginia and West Virginia, and I used his jurisdiction to cross state lines."

According to Hatfield, Putnam came across as a guy who'd always wanted to be a police officer, the kind of guy who would never be satisfied with a nine-to-five job. He needed to do something with a little "zip," otherwise he'd be bored to death. And he was ambitious about his career. Putnam wanted to move up as quickly as possible, the deputy thought.

"He was using my knowledge of the people. I

had information on Cat Eyes, and we wanted to get those robberies solved," Hatfield said. "I spent a lot of time with him. He was the kind of guy who kept on working, putting in the extra hours. I went with Mark to Home Creek, Virginia. This was before I introduced him to Susan Smith. We went there because Mark had a hot lead after a bank had been robbed. We went to a car lot over in Buchanan County, and discovered that Cat Eyes had purchased a Firebird and paid five thousand dollars in cash for it. He'd also purchased a second car with cash. Then we went over to the Richlands Mall in Virginia and found out that Cat Eyes had bought a lot of expensive jewelry there, so we were on to him."

Still, everything Hatfield and Putnam had picked up was only circumstantial evidence. They had been unable to obtain the proof they needed to indict and convict Cat Eyes Lockhart, but Hatfield assured Putnam that Susan Smith had been an effective informant of his for years, and he thought she would probably prove to be fruitful in this instance. Informants were hard to come by unless you had something to threaten them with, and since Susan was in no kind of trouble, Putnam figured it would be difficult to get her cooperation. Hatfield assured Putnam that Susan would work with him if the FBI would make it profitable enough for her.

He stressed her knowledge of drug trafficking, and he said she could also find out about other criminal activities — bank robberies, burglaries, and things of that nature. Smith had helped him for three or four years, on and off, he said, and she was the one who just might be able to hand Cat Eyes over to them. Putnam told Hatfield to offer Susan five thousand dollars for information leading to Cat Eyes' arrest.

"She ran in a circle of people who did anything they wanted, pulled off all kinds of things; and she could get information out of anybody. That was just her way," Hatfield later said. "She had done me many favors, but in our department, we don't have a lot of money to pay informants, so when this offer from Putnam came up, Susan and I talked about setting her up as an FBI informant so she could receive more money."

Susan's ex-husband Kenneth was with her the day she met Putnam in a hospital parking lot in Williamson, West Virginia, about fifteen minutes from the Freeburn/Vulcan area. Susan would remember the day well. Kenneth gave her a hard time for flirting with the handsome FBI man, and she would later tell Shelby that she was bowled over by Mark's charm and sophistication. Putnam had a refined New England manner of speech, and he kidded about her Southern accent during their initial meeting.

It was on that hot summer night in the Williamson Memorial Hospital parking lot, just after Putnam had finished interviewing Kenneth, that the chemistry between Mark and Susan flared.

But Susan had her doubts about cooperating. For one thing, she wasn't sure he was going to come across with the money. Others in Freeburn had been promised money by the feds, and then had been "cheated" out of it. That was what she had always heard. And even if Putnam would pay her, she wasn't sure she should get involved with him. She knew Cat Eyes would kill her if he found out he was being ratted on. She didn't know if it was worth the risk. Still, this handsome man was avidly pursuing her, and she was overwhelmed.

Kenneth had gotten out of Putnam's car moments before, he was shaking his head in a manner that told her to keep her mouth shut, so she was scared. And besides, five thousand dollars wasn't all that much money . . . she might make that in a few drug transactions with Kenneth and their Chicago connections. What was Putnam offering that would make it worth her while? Susan wondered. But sometime during their introductory hour of flirting and carrying on, it suddenly seemed clear, that Putnam was offering her something much more than money.

Kenneth remembers thinking that Susan was getting too close to Mark during the interview that night. He saw too much laughing and cutting up, and he believed that something was going on between them from the very minute they met. It enraged him to see how Susan behaved with Putnam. Fueled by anger and jealousy, Kenneth finally turned to Hatfield and said, "Hey, what's taking them so long in there? Is this the way the FBI operates?"

But Hatfield just shrugged.

When Susan emerged from Putnam's car, all smiles, she told Hatfield that she and Mark had come to an "understanding." Of course, right away Kenneth didn't like the idea of Susan becoming involved with Putnam. He could see that she was smitten with the agent, and he knew that her becoming an informant would put their present existence in jeopardy. But he kept silent until Putnam and Hatfield were out of sight.

On the drive back home, Kenneth and Susan got into an argument that was so fervent Susan insisted Kenneth drop her off in front of Shelby's house in Freeburn. She said she didn't want to be around him or any of his seedy friends in Vulcan. But before he let her out of the car, Kenneth continued to yell at her, trying to bully her into staying away from Putnam.

"I don't want you messing with this FBI bastard. What do you think you're going to pull off? Don't you think Cat will get suspicious?"

"Hey, don't you go telling me what to do! This is my life, Kenneth! If you don't want to work with the FBI, fine, but it's none of your damn business what I do, you understand, because I need the money, okay! So just stay the hell out of it."

"What the fuck are you going to do when you get caught in the middle?"

"Look, Kenneth, I don't have to worry about nothing! This guy is going to protect me. What do you think? The FBI doesn't let you get hurt when you're working for them!"

"Bullshit!" Kenneth taunted.

"I'll get Cat Eyes in the back. That's going to get me five thousand dollars! So why don't you just keep your mouth shut!"

"Oh, hell, you go do whatever you want to, Susan. If you want to be a stupid bitch and trust that guy, then go do it. I don't know what you're thinking, that you're going to get laid I guess!"

"Oh, shut up, Kenneth! Why don't you just shut your mouth! This is business now! This is no fooling around!"

With that, Kenneth took off for Vulcan and Susan went over to Shelby's. She told her sister all about Mark Putnam, about how handsome he was and what a great body he had. Insisting that she was going to help him solve a bank robbery case, that she was going to get paid five thousand dollars, she vowed that she would get Mark Putnam to fall in love with her.

"I really hardly paid any attention to her when she came in talking to me about Mark Putnam that night," Shelby recalls. "Susan just rambled on about so much that you got to a point where you just didn't pay attention to what she was saying. She'd make up so many stories and claim she knew so many different things about people, and half of it wasn't true. You just never knew what to believe."

Meanwhile, as the two law enforcement men

drove back to Pikeville in Hatfield's police car, Hatfield was deliberate in explaining the problem Susan might pose, telling Putnam that Susan was the type of girl who "fabricated," someone who was insecure about her personal life and who would make up stories about having affairs with important people. He warned Putnam to be "cautious" with her. He said that Susan was streetwise, that though she wasn't an educated person, she was sharp in a lot of ways and Mark might find himself in her clutches if he didn't watch himself.

But Putnam just shrugged the warnings off.

"I tried to explain the situation to him going in, because he was young, he was new to it," Hatfield remembers. "He was a good agent, he loved what he was doing, but he needed to be careful around Susan. She had ways of manipulating people. She was good at it. But I don't know if Mark listened to me. You know, he just said yeah, yeah, yeah."

Burt Hatfield knew what he was talking about when it came to Susan Smith because he'd had a special personal relationship with her over the years. Hatfield claims that they shared a father/daughter type friendship. Whatever the case, the two of them talked a lot, and Susan would use Hatfield's shoulder to cry on. Whenever she would help him with information about local criminals, Hatfield would listen to her talk about her life, about Kenneth, and about her depression. Hatfield thought drugs played a part in Susan's willingness to talk so freely about her personal life.

"Kenneth was a bum, an alcoholic, a drug user," Hatfield said, "and she was always talking about Kenneth laying drunk. I'd tell her, if she wasn't happy in the situation, she needed to get out of it. I'd tell her it's not going to get any better. I'd say, why don't you move, either backwards or forwards would be better than just staying there."

But rather than taking Hatfield's words to heart, Susan would construct tales about an incredible love life, telling Hatfield about all the assorted men who were in love with her. That was Susan's usual response whenever Hatfield questioned her about how things were going with Kenneth. She would talk about important men in Pikeville, say she was sleeping with them, say she was getting paid a lot of money for her sexual favors. The Pike County Deputy didn't believe Susan, but occasionally he would check one of her stories out, only to catch her in another lie.

The affair between Susan Daniels Smith and Mark Stevens Putnam had begun with Susan seducing Mark in his car, which was parked near a deserted strip mine just outside town. Soon, they became routine, these drives to remote hill areas, and on these forays out past civilization, Mark would tell Susan about the cases he had worked on since his arrival in Pikeville and he'd talk about his days as a soccer player and at prep school. Ironically, although it probably was true that Susan was the one who pushed their involvement along, it was Mark who stood to gain the most from the affair. He was using Susan as a stepping stone to further his career.

From the moment their sexual relationship began, Susan diligently pursued discussions with Cat Eyes, acting as though she herself were interested in robbing banks, asking about his various criminal techniques. Night after night, she would pump him for information without Cat Eyes ever suspecting that she was turning every bit of it right over to Putnam.

Mark had given Susan his home number and had told her to call him day or night, even at four A.M., if she found out anything that would indicate Cat Eyes was about to pull off a bank heist. In the meantime, her relationship with Kenneth was growing increasingly stormy, characterized by more and more fights. It blew hot and cold, with Susan running increasingly into Mark Putnam's arms, having established a love affair with the FBI man just weeks after they began working together.

Putnam, who ordinarily was in complete control of himself, lost his self-possession in this case. Drawn in by Susan's childlike awe of him, he never lost sight of the fact that he needed her to get this job done. It was a complex situation, but he was perfectly capable of putting on an act for Kathy and his co-workers, who did not suspect he would be involved with the likes of Susan Smith, a girl from the hills with no education. The clash in their backgrounds was the perfect alibi for him. In fact, Kathy had even seen Susan going in and out of Mark's office on more than one occasion, according to Susan's brother, Billy Joe, who had watched the two women exchange nods and glances.

Naturally, when Susan began telling Hatfield that she and Mark were in love with each other, that they were spending nights together, Hatfield never believed her. But in time, as Susan began to talk openly about her affair with Putnam, Hatfield questioned his colleague about the relationship, using a joking manner to disguise the gravity of the situation.

"Hey, Mark, you dating Susan? She says you are," he casually remarked.

"Ah, hell, you know she always says those things," Putnam responded. "She said she's screwing you, Burt. She said she's screwing Ron Poole. She said she's screwing another guy that works over at the federal building. You know how she is. You can't take her seriously."

"Yeah, I just thought I'd ask. For the hell of it, you know. She talks about you a lot."

"Oh, really?"

Putnam spoke convincingly, never letting Hatfield see that he and Susan were involved in an intense sexual relationship.

As the weeks passed, Susan spent more and more time in Pikeville, telling her family in Freeburn about her romance with Mark but not yet giving them any information about his wife's frequent absences. She kept quiet about that because she was afraid that if Kenneth found out Mark's wife had left town, the situation would be explosive and everything would backfire on her. Susan was smart enough to know that she could not afford to lose her family over someone who was just casually involved with her. She also knew that she had to continue to satisfy Kenneth's needs, and for a long time, at least for a year, neither Mark nor Susan were found out by their respective mates.

From the beginning of their affair, Mark continued his life as a family man, and things were going well for him. Kathy was six months pregnant and was making regular trips to see her doctor in Connecticut, so she was relatively happy, and Mark continued to take Danielle out on "dates." But, all the while, he saw Susan, meeting her in the afternoons, making passionate love to her, and afterward pumping her for information about Cat Eyes. And whenever Kathy took Danielle to Connecticut, Susan and Mark's times together would be more frequent and prolonged. It was a suitable arrangement.

Back in Vulcan, Susan was still busy with her children, getting their clothes laid out each morning for the school day, cooking meals for Kenneth and the rest, and making life as bearable as possible for herself by continuing to use and sell drugs. Cat Eyes, she believed, was about to pull off another robbery, so she had Mark on the telephone constantly, reporting his every move. Cat Eyes was hanging out with a rowdy bunch in a placed called Williamson Lunch, and Susan was sure he was meeting his soon-to-be bank robber accomplices there.

And then it happened.

It was on September 10, 1987, that Cat Eyes Lockhart, accompanied by an unidentified man, entered the Ferrells Creek branch of the First National Bank of Pikeville, in Belcher, Kentucky. A ski mask over his face, he handed a pillowcase to the teller, instructing her to fill it up with money and not to put any dye packs in. He then herded all the bank employees and the customers into the vault area of the bank, again telling the teller not to put any dye packs into the bag, at which time he reached down and took one dye pack out of the pillowcase.

He absconded with over twelve thousand dollars, which included prerecorded "bait" bills, but when he got outside the bank, a dye pack exploded just before he drove off in a white van, heading toward an area called Mouthcard, Kentucky, where individuals saw the van whiz past a service station en route to the Virginia state line.

The bank had already been staked out by Mark Putnam, Dan Brennan, and the Kentucky State Police, thanks to Susan's detailed information, But, unfortunately, no police were on the scene at the time of the robbery. The day before Cat Eyes hit, however, Putnam had instructed a bank teller to insert a pack of one hundred two-dollar bills and a red dye pack into

Cat Eyes' pillowcase. These would later be used as evidence against the robber.

The van was found parked on a gravel road about fifteen minutes after the robbery, a shotgun left inside along with two hundred twenty dollars worth of red-stained money. Photographs were taken of the tire impressions left near the van, and Dan Brennan observed that it looked as though it had been struck by a small gray vehicle. He found damage on the right rear side of the van and noticed that a hub cap had come off. The next day, Brennan summoned Putnam to accompany him to Buchanan County, Virginia, where they examined a gray four-door Dodge Colt resembling the car seen near the bank, which, it turned out, belonged to Cat Eyes Lockhart. Just one week after the robbery, a man fitting Cat Eyes' description entered the Pikeville National Bank to exchange one hundred seventy-two dollars in two-dollar bills, some of which had red dye on them, for other currency.

When the bank teller identified Lockhart as the man who had exchanged the two-dollar bills, Dan Brennan arrested and interrogated him. During the questioning Cat Eyes told Brennan that he had sold a stereo to an individual named Bishop at a roadside stand in Belfry, Kentucky, receiving two-dollar bills in payment.

According to Pike County Records, a preliminary hearing was held on September 24, 1987, and Lockhart's lawyer indicated the defendant would testify that he obtained the two-dollar bills from two strangers for work done on their Cadillac. Brennan then testified as to the statements Lockhart made about selling a stereo. Based on Lockhart's prior statement, his testimony during the pretrial hearing was impeached and Cat Eyes Lockhart was indicted by a grand jury in October of 1987 for taking twelve thousand eight hundred seven dollars from the Ferrells Creek branch of the First National Bank of Pikeville.

Lockhart's trial would take place in London, Kentucky, on January 27, 1988, and Susan and Kenneth Smith, along with their neighbor, Gary Mounts, and Cat Eyes' uncle, MacArthur Lockhart, were all summoned as witnesses.

Gary Mounts, who grew up with Cat Eyes and Kenneth, was called because he'd happened to give Cat Eyes a lift up the road in Vulcan on the day of the robbery. Putnam and Brennan had approached Mounts about this on several occasions, and Mounts recalls that Putnam was a down-to-earth type of guy, and he says their interview went well, although Mounts contends he had no real information to offer the agent.

"Well, did you pick Cat Eyes up on the morning of September tenth in Vulcan?" Putnam wanted to know.

"I picked him up one morning in Vulcan with a duffle bag. I don't know what morning it was. He walked on the road every day. It was an everyday thing to give him a ride. That's all I can tell you," Mounts said.

That answer wasn't good enough, so for the second time Putnam and Brennan went to question Mounts. This time they had a summons with them, and they wanted him to go to Pikeville to be fingerprinted. Mounts told them he had nothing to hide, and after some arguing, he went along and got fingerprinted. About two weeks later, the FBI team appeared with a summons for Mounts to testify against Cat Eyes in court. Mounts kept insisting that he knew nothing, that he wasn't involved in the bank robbery, but his pleas were of no use. Putnam pressured Mounts into testifying in London, claiming that Mounts might be cited as an accessory to the crime if he didn't cooperate.

"What are you handing me a summons for?" Mounts asked, fearful.

"Well some of that bank money came up with your fingerprints on it," Putnam told him.

"No. That's where you're wrong, buddy. Show me the money. Show me proof!"

"It's in London. You'll see it when you get there. Your expenses are paid. You've got a place to sleep. Come prepared to stay two or three days," Putnam said before he drove off.

So Gary Mounts went to London with Susan and Kenneth, sharing a room with MacArthur Lockhart. Actually, the four of them shared adjoining rooms, a suite. They had quite an exclusive setup, Susan thought, and just minutes after they arrived, Mark called her room and wanted to know if everybody was all right.

Kenneth grabbed the receiver and asked,

"Hey, how can we find any beer around here?"

"It's a dry county. You'll have to go about forty miles to Tennessee. Are you planning on going?"

"Yeah."

"Well, be back in two hours, cause I gotta keep a check on you," Putnam said in an authoritative tone.

So the four of them went down to Jellico, Tennessee, an eighty-mile round trip, to pick up two cases of beer and a few bags of ice. However, much to their surprise, when they returned to the Ramada Inn Putnam told them that none of their testimony would be needed that day, that they had made a wasted trip. They would be called back, they were told, when the trial was rescheduled. So they loaded their beer in the trunk and traveled the four hours back to Freeburn.

Upon his return to Freeburn, Mounts discovered that the FBI never paid the Ramada bill. He alleges that for weeks to follow, Agent Putnam was trying to stick him with the tab for the motel room.

"You better pay this, or they'll put you in jail," Putnam threatened on one of his visits to Mounts, waving the bill in his hand.

"Well, buddy, I was a witness for the prosecution, and you told me you were going to pay it, that everything would be taken care of. Then I got down there and it was a different situation. I'm not out anything, and I'm not going to be out anything—because I don't know any-

100

thing!" Mounts told him.

Putnam showed up again in Freeburn two weeks later, and when he spotted Mounts across the river in Vulcan, he blocked the Vulcan bridge with his car. Putnam was driving a four wheel-drive pickup truck, a copper-tone Ford '78 or '79 model, Mounts recalled, and Putnam cornered him, saying, "We're going down here and cash this check. I've got to take this money to the people at the motel. You're messing up the witness program."

So Gary Mounts signed a government check at a West Virginia bank, arguing all the while that Putnam had promised to pay for the room in the first place, that the FBI was responsible for the problem.

A few weeks later, Susan and Kenneth and Gary were summoned to appear in London, Kentucky, once again. And this time Mark instructed them not to leave their rooms, not to communicate with anybody, and to order their meals from room service.

The Ramada in London is a large brick structure with white columns adorning the entranceway. Its restaurant even serves shellfish, rare in most establishments in the vicinity. Since Susan Smith had never actually been on a vacation in her life, she was in her glory in London. She had a beautiful room to sleep in, fancy food being brought to her bedside, and Mark, her lover, was staying right down the hall.

Mounts didn't know that Susan was working as an FBI informant at the time. During his

101

three-day stay in London, he didn't understand the FBI man's overly friendly behavior with her. He recalls that Susan wore a see-through pink negligee when she went to talk to Putnam before the trial started, which struck him as quite odd.

"I thought he was letting her get a little bit too friendly with him, and I kind of suspected that something was going on between them because she flirted with Putnam right in front of me and Kenneth," Mounts said. "Then before the trial, Putnam wanted each of us to come down to his room separately, to go over the questions, and I went down for maybe fifteen minutes, Kenneth was with him about five minutes, but Suzie stayed with him over an hour."

But Kenneth had no proof that Mark and Susan were involved in a love affair. She vehemently denied all of his accusations, acting insulted that he could think an FBI man would violate federal rules. She had her ex-husband convinced that the extent of her involvement with Mark was the undercover operation, and she told Kenneth that she spent the extra time in Mark's motel room going over her orchestrated testimony, which, she reminded him, Gary Mounts was to have no knowledge of, under any circumstances.

Each morning after the trial began, Mark Putnam escorted Mr. and Mrs. Smith and Mr. Mounts over to the federal courthouse, a beautiful old building in downtown London. The courtroom, located on the second floor, is trimmed in mahogany and marked by an oval shape. Its oval dropped ceiling and arched windows lend it a touch of elegance. Beyond that, however, the room has an air of authority about it, which is compounded by the heavy security checks routinely taking place at the door, everyone passing through a metal detector and opening all bags for inspection.

When Susan was called and sworn in as a government witness, she sat in a large box to the right of the judge and spoke her name clearly into the microphone. Mark Putnam, Kenneth Smith, Gary Mounts, and the others looked on as she pointed out Carl "Cat Eyes" Lockhart. Susan stated for the record that exhibit 3, a single-barreled gun, looked exactly like the weapon Cat Eyes Lockhart had kept in a pillowcase at her home. This was believed to be the gun Cat Eyes had used to pull off the bank robbery at the Ferrells Creek branch. When asked about her knowledge of the bank robbery, Susan told the court that Cat Eyes and Sherri Justice appeared at her home at about eleven P.M. on Friday, a week before the First National Bank of Pikeville was robbed, at which time they talked about their plans to rob a bank.

Before Susan left the stand, she was asked whether or not any law enforcement officers had come to her home after September 10, investigating the robbery in question. She responded that the investigation began before September 10, that Burt Hatfield had come to her house once and that Mark Putnam had also come there to talk about the bank situation. When she brought up Putnam's name in connection with the investigation before September 10, the prosecutor cut her off. "That's all," he said, and Susan stepped down and was excused.

On January 28, 1988, at the US District Court, Cat Eyes was convicted and sentenced to serve fifty-seven years in federal prison. Susan watched as the one hundred ninety-five pound bearded man with the strange hazel-blue eyes was marched off in handcuffs. He was taken to the Fayette County Metro Detention Center in Lexington, Kentucky, where, he claims, Mark Putnam came to see him in March of 1988. Putnam was there to try to get Cat Eyes to "roll over" on his partners, Lockhart said. Cat Eyes alleges that Putnam asked a lot of questions about Susan—about the time she spent in Chicago and Louisiana—and seemed overly interested in her.

Years later, Cat Eyes told others that he was in love with Susan and to this day, from his jail cell in Leavenworth, Kansas, the bank robber claims that Susan was acting on Kenneth's instructions. Still refusing to distrust Susan, he claims that the two of them might have become lovers if it weren't for Putnam's interference.

Chapter Six

Upon their return from London, Susan and Mark continued their secret liaison, but now rumors about them began to spread. Most people who heard the stories wondered why Putnam would cheat on his wife. Kathy was so beautiful and elegant that Susan hardly matched up. By now Putnam had a new FBI partner, Special Agent Ron Poole. Poole had become aware that some kind of hanky-panky was going on, and he had noticed Mark and Susan kissing and hugging over at the FBI office. And others at the federal building on Main Street had seen the two of them acting like teenagers, Susan sitting on Mark's desk and holding his hand while he read through FBI paperwork.

Even though that kind of entanglement is prohibited by FBI rules and regulations — having sex with an informant would be grounds for dismissal — Mark and Susan carried on, much to the chagrin of the federal office workers around them. Sometimes, Susan would hang around in the lobby until Mark arrived. At others she appeared unannounced, and when Mark walked into his office, she would rush in with him. The two reportedly spent many hours behind closed doors.

Sometimes Mark left his office door open, and he and Susan just talked and kidded around. Whenever Susan's brother, Billy Joe, waited for her in the lobby of the federal building, he would see the two of them teasing and touching each other. It was a regular routine. Billy Joe couldn't understand what Susan saw in Putnam, but he knew she was doing a good job of feeding Mark's ego. Susan was Putnam's number-one fan.

Billy Joe "Bo" Daniels was now living with Susan in Vulcan. He'd been there when Susan made collect calls to the FBI office. He'd heard her call Mark Putnam's house. In early 1988, Susan was having lengthy conversations with the FBI man on a daily basis. Billy Joe was all too familiar with Mark Putnam. Putnam had an unhappy marriage, he knew. His wife resented living in Appalachia. Billy Joe had heard the story over and over while driving his sister over to Pikeville to see Mark.

In fact, throughout 1988, Billy Joe had become Susan's regular driver to and from Pikeville. Carmella, his girlfriend at that time, recorded thirty-two trips to Pikeville in her diary. They would drop Susan off behind the courthouse, and she would spend hours with

Putnam, always returning with a big smile on her face and her clothes rumpled. Kenneth still didn't know what was going on, but he was suspicious and Susan constantly had to make up excuses in order to leave the house and go meet Mark.

The road from Freeburn to Pikeville is treacherous. Narrow, it winds around the mountains, a cliff usually on one side and a creek often on the other. The signs read, "Caution, Trucks Entering the Highway," and unfortunately the passing coal trucks are outnumbered only by the hundreds of railroad cars which cross at five different locations, all filled with gloomy black heaps which obliterate the view of the hills.

Billy Joe and Susan knew the road well. They had traveled it for a year and a half so Susan could keep her rendezvous with Mark. Upon their return to Vulcan, they'd come into the house spouting lies about what they'd been doing all day, and for a long time, Kenneth was fooled. He believed that Susan was doing informant work or that Billy Joe had doctor appointments to keep or business to take care of over at Pikeville.

In the early stages of Susan's affair with Mark, Bo Daniels brought his girlfriend, Carmella, with him on the drives to Pikeville. The pair would drop Susan off and then rent a room at the Pinson Motel downtown, staying there for about two or three hours while Mark and Susan went off someplace, usually to a vacant strip mine or a cheap motel outside town.

Although Bo didn't like the idea of his sister being used, he never questioned her about her involvement with Putnam. He felt she knew what she was doing, and he believed she could take care of herself. Besides, she was making good money, often returning with two or three hundred dollars after a meeting with the FBI man. And Susan was always generous with the cash, handing Bo a hundred dollars to make the trips worth his while.

Carmella was only fifteen at the time and had no business traipsing off to Pikeville, much less sleeping with Bo at a motel. She had met Susan in October of 1987, just after Bo had moved into the Vulcan house. Out of necessity, Susan had told her about Mark Putnam, but she had made her swear not to tell anybody about the affair. Carmella said she always "covered" for Susan, never telling anybody about the constant trips to Pikeville.

Time after time, Carmella and Bo would take Susan to the same meeting place—the parking lot behind the county courthouse. Susan would wait in Bo's Datsun 240 Z, and it would usually take Mark just five minutes to show. He'd always be wearing sunglasses, and he'd throw his hand up and wave. But he never did speak to Billy Joe Daniels or his pretty blond girlfriend. The minute Putnam's brown car appeared, Susan would jump into it and they would take off, Susan having told Bo when to pick her up at the lot. Carmella remembers many occasions when

Susan would get back into Bo's car and say, "Lord, I had the best time there ever was today! Me and Mark spent the whole day together! We've been in a motel all day!"

Although Susan never said which motel they frequented, she did make references that indicated it was a tacky one, often calling Mark cheap. It was later discovered that Putnam was taking Susan to the Goldenrod Motel, a tiny unkempt place which sits directly across from the Pikeville Kentucky State Police post.

Usually when Susan returned to the courthouse parking lot, Bo was angry because she'd been gone much longer than she had promised. He knew he would have to make excuses to Carmella's mom, not to mention Kenneth, who would hound him for information about their whereabouts as soon as they walked through the door. Susan always left home dressed casually for her trips to Pikeville, wearing blue jeans, tennis shoes, and simple cotton shirts or sweaters most of the time. She intentionally underdressed so as not to arouse Kenneth's suspicion, but on the way over in the car, she put on jewelry, makeup, and high heels for her encounters with Mark.

When the threesome got back to the Tug Valley area, they'd drop Carmella off at her mom's place, up Smith Fork at Phelps. Then, in the evening, Bo would return to Smith Fork and bring Carmella up to Vulcan to visit. Carmella had explicit instructions not to say a word to Kenneth about having been in Pikeville that day, and she always played along. Still, she never could understand how Susan got away with the deception.

"How do you do it? How do you get by with it?" she'd ask her when they were by themselves.

"It's hard. When I'm working with the FBI on something, I tell Kenneth I have to go to Pikeville, but I have to be careful that I don't slip and say something about Mark because Kenneth'd have a fit. You know, I still sleep with Kenneth sometimes."

"And he can't tell anything's different?"

"No, he thinks I'm going over with Bo on business. A lot of times Bo makes something up, says he's going to trade his car in or whatever." Susan laughed.

Many times Susan and Bo went into the bathroom to discuss their excuse for another trip to Pikeville. Susan had to find ways to make Kenneth believe she was still faithful to him. It was the only way she could keep some peace in the house.

These trips went on throughout the whole of 1988, and by mid year, Susan made one thing clear to everyone around her: she was willing to risk everything—her life, her kids, her home—to be with Mark. She was obsessed with him and pursued him unabashedly, bragging to everyone about his movie-star looks, worshiping his FBI status. Perhaps she had hooked him because she knew exactly how to satisfy his ego, and she told Shelby, along with intimate details about their sex life, that she was certain

Mark couldn't live without her.

That Putnam was making love to her in order to trap bank robbers never crossed Susan's mind. He called her several times a day and always said "I love you," before hanging up. "I love you, too," Bo would hear Susan say, that is, when Kenneth wasn't around.

With Kenneth, Susan continued to lead an alternate existence, giving most people the impression that she was a homebody who was devoted to her "husband" and her children. Now that she had some cash coming in, she cooked big meals and dressed herself and her kids in brand-new clothing purchased at fashionable boutiques in Matewan or Williamson. And she was improving her home, acquiring Colonial-style furniture and dressing the place up with brand-new curtains and costly silk flower arrangements.

Once Mark Putnam had entered Susan's life, however, no matter how much she fixed things up, her house didn't seem adequate. As the affair continued, things were becoming more and more unbearable for Susan at the Smith household. Her biggest gripe was that the house sat directly on the gravel side of the railroad track and trains constantly went by, making screeching noises which increasingly began to grate on her nerves. She especially hated the sounds now that they were interfering with her telephone conversations with Mark. It was always an embarrassment when a train passed by and she had to hang up on Putnam and wait fifteen minutes

111

or so for the screeching to die down before she called him back.

And the trains at Vulcan now started to embarrass her in other ways. She had become self-conscious about the dust the railroad cars kicked up, covering her house and yard with black particles day in and out. Every morning, she got up and wet down the large chunks of gravel in her front yard so the dust wouldn't kick up as much, just in case Mark happened to stop by. She sprayed her house too, washing it clean of black soot. And of course she also had to wash Bo's car, to keep it shiny for her drives to Pikeville.

By the summer of 1988, Kenneth had spread the news about Susan's work with the FBI in an attempt to get her to stop seeing Mark. Kenneth was now almost certain they were having an affair, and he figured that when enough people in the community found her out, Susan would get scared and would stop running around with Putnam.

But Kenneth's plan backfired. Susan spent increasingly more time in Pikeville, keeping as much distance between herself and the people in Freeburn as possible, and she began to make it clear that the only reason she remained in Vulcan was the children. The couple began to argue in front of the children whenever she returned from Pikeville. Kenneth called her names, he made accusations, and Susan told him how much she loathed him.

She now had money coming in from a few

sources — drug dealing, welfare, and the FBI. She brought home enough to make ends meet. But because of her drug habit — she was a chronic cocaine user and took large doses of prescription medications — she never seemed to have any extra cash to spend on her kids.

Compounding her difficulties, she was having trouble collecting all of the money she'd been promised for her informant work. She had made about nine or ten thousand dollars in almost two years as an informant, which is not very much. At some point in mid 1988, Susan went to see a Pikeville attorney, Kelsey Friend, Jr. Friend remembers that she was very hard up for money at the time. She told him that she hadn't been paid as much as she'd been told she would get for her part in the Cat Eyes' case, that the FBI hadn't made it worth her while. Susan wanted Friend's advice about being compensated for the balance.

"Do you think I can trust the FBI to pay?" she asked Friend.

"Why, sure you can. If they offered you a million dollars, they would pay you," the attorney told her.

"Well, the situation is that I've had to testify, and this is really a dangerous situation, and the only thing I want to know is I'm not going to be set up in this, because it's already been months since the trial and I haven't been paid!"

"I can assure you, if the FBI promised you something, it will be done," Friend insisted.

On another visit to Friend's office, Susan

asked the attorney questions about the federal witness protection program, such as getting a new identity and social security number. At that point, she seemed nervous and worried about her own dealings with the FBI. Friend had no idea that she was romantically involved with Agent Putnam or that she probably could give him some advice about FBI matters.

The attorney described Susan as a "come-on" type, who made advances and let him know that she was available. He said Susan always came into his office all dolled up, heavily perfumed, and wearing a lot of makeup. Friend believed she could have feigned the appearance any prospective date would have wanted. "I think she was a chameleon. She would strike me as being somebody from Lexington, you know, she was cultured and sophisticated, not at all like somebody from Matewan," he recalled.

Friend claims Susan came to his office often and complained to him about her hard life with Kenneth. The attorney got the impression that she was trying to "solicit" him. Aid to Dependent Children, she said, was her sole means of support, and Kenneth was abusive toward her. They were just living together for lack of housing. Their marriage was over, she declared.

"I need money, you know. Kenneth's not working. Kenneth's not bringing in anything. I've got to pay my phone bill. Kenneth won't do anything. We could go off and have a good time. I've got a whole bunch of bills to pay," according to Friend, Susan carried on like this on more than one occasion.

Evidently, Kelsey Friend, Jr., had no reason to question Susan Smith's willingness to work with Mark Putnam and sell out her friends. He said he never once suspected Mark Putnam of any wrongdoing. It was Susan he distrusted. The area she was from had always been known as a "badlands, where people were usually out of control and abusive toward one another." That she was working as an informant seemed normal for someone from Freeburn. Susan didn't seem any different from other informers he had talked to. She was ruthless, he thought, just out to get money.

"The mountain belt is a different world. We all know everybody's business, and it's not unusual for somebody to inform the law about a crime. The people who are out committing crimes know it's highly possible that someone will tell on them. It's a chance they know they're taking," Friend explained.

But the idea that Susan Smith and Mark Putnam were having an affair was beyond the comprehension of Friend or any other prominent Pikeville citizen. These people knew the pair had a working relationship, but they assumed any rumors about a love affair would prove false.

Susan continued to work with Mark Putnam and proved to be quite an effective informant. Her reputation with lawmen grew stronger, and she became friendly with local deputies and walked around Pikeville with her head held high, living on the "right" side of the law for once in her life. Somehow she blocked out the reality that she still used and sold drugs, and that she turned her "contacts" over to the FBI. This part of her life never bothered her. She was only concerned with impressing Mark, and she believed that her lover approved of her actions and her lifestyle.

During this time, Susan was trying to establish a relationship with Kathy Putnam by means of the telephone, asking her about Mark and their children. The two women sometimes talked for hours, Susan telling Kathy about Kenneth, her kids, her PMS, just anything to keep the conversation going. Kathy later told an interviewer that she was familiar with all of Mark's cases, with all of his informants, and it was not out of the ordinary to get calls from informants at home.

What was out of the ordinary, however, were Susan's insinuations that she loved Mark, that she would do anything for him, and that she was sleeping with him. But Kathy apparently didn't believe Susan. She felt sorry for this young woman who had such a miserable life, and would listen as Susan poured her heart out. Repeatedly, Susan told Kathy that Miranda and Brady needed clothes, that she didn't have enough money to feed them. Sometimes Susan threatened to kill herself. Sometimes she said she was hopelessly in love with Mark. Once, she kept Kathy on the phone from ten P.M. to four A.M.

Meanwhile, Susan asked Mark if Kathy suspected anything, and he assured her that Kathy was trusting and did not question his relationships with other women. He had many women "friends," he said, and Kathy knew about them. She wasn't the jealous type. Susan often hinted that Mark could leave his wife, hoping he would say he'd get a divorce, but he usually contended that, while he wanted to leave Kathy, he had to stay with her for the sake of the children. At times, however, he let Susan think he might leave Kathy. Then she would run back to her friends and report that Mark was in love with her, that he was going to marry her. "He's rich, Suzie. He's not going to leave his wife for a girl from around here," her friends would say, but Susan paid no attention to them.

And Mark did remain with his family. In fact, he would tell other cops that Kathy's father had promised to buy them a house worth a quarter of a million dollars. Putnam even bragged that he could leave the FBI and be set for life in his father-in-law's business, but he loved his work.

Putnam did find happiness in being an FBI man. He worked hard at keeping himself in top condition and making high scores at target-practice sessions in Lexington. On many occasions, he went over to Harmon's Branch, just outside Pikeville, to the public shooting range used by a lot of the local cops. There he practiced his shooting skills.

No doubt, Putnam took his FBI work to

heart and relished the fact that he could cross boundaries other law enforcement men couldn't. He was proud of the power he had as a G-man, and he boasted to Susan that he could go undercover and walk into dope houses without being suspected. He even bragged that he could talk any kind of criminal into cooperating because of his ability to become just like one of them. Mark was filled with machismo, and Susan ate his words up.

Susan kept herself ultra thin for Mark. She rarely ate, hanging on to the fervent hope that something magical would happen, that Mark would dump Kathy and she could take her place at his side. Susan knew she didn't match up to Mark's standards as far as education was concerned, but she tried her best to become more like him. Whenever she spoke with Mark, friends recall, she carefully enunciated every word, careful not to let him hear any leftover "hillbilly" drawl. Perhaps Susan figured she could win Mark over ultimately by emulating and idolizing him. She knew his ego needed stroking and Kathy wasn't doing that.

In the meantime, Susan's family began to fear for her safety, often questioning her about her "work" with Mark and what kind of trouble it might get her into. "Aren't you afraid you might get killed?" Shelby asked, but Susan just laughed and promised that Mark had her fully protected.

"Ain't nothing going to happen to me as long as I'm working with them!" Susan told her sister. "Mark even told me I could deal drugs all I wanted, and if I got caught, he would get me out of it!"

"What? You believe that?" Shelby sneered.

"It's the God's truth, Shelb. He told me I could deal coke or whatever I wanted, and it would be okay."

"You sure about that, Suzie? That don't sound right."

"Shelb, the man goes and takes coke out of the FBI safe himself."

"Oh, yeah, right, and you believe him?" Shelby snickered.

"I saw him do it once, Shelb! I got mad at him one time because he kept saying Kathy wanted coke all the time, and I told him I wanted some and he wouldn't give me any. Then I told him to just let me see it, so I could taste it, you know, to see if it was the real thing."

"And he let you?"

"Hell, yes! He even tried some of it with me!"

"Okay, so this big FBI man uses coke? Suzie, come on. You've got to be lying!"

"No, he doesn't really use it. He just tried it that one time. It's his wife that's got a habit. I mean, I don't know it for sure, but that's what he tells me."

"Well, don't kid yourself and think you can just go around trying to bust people and not get found out! And when they do, there'll be hell to pay, Suzie!"

Susan told Shelby about one of her adventures in trying to bust a big drug dealer, explaining how Putnam wired her, feeling her breasts as he did it, and then sent her into a Pikeville mansion where she was to try to make a cocaine purchase. Susan said she complained that the wire hurt her ribs, but that didn't stop Putnam from continuing to use her in an attempt to tape the drug dealers in and around Pike County.

Throughout 1988, Susan made many attempts to bust people for selling drugs, sometimes entering the offices of prominent businesses in Pikeville all wired up, but unfortunately, she never had much luck. It seems she was most beneficial to Mark when it came to bank robberies, not drug deals, but that was okay with him. That was really all he needed Susan for anyway. He had other informants who successfully helped him with drug busts.

At one point, Susan claimed she went back to the FBI office with a bag of pills she'd bought from one of the East Kentucky sheriffs. Agent Ron Poole later arrested four eastern Kentucky sheriffs during a crackdown on local law enforcement. So it seems Susan Smith was, for a while, a part of the "team." She also contributed the information about a group headed by MacArthur Lockhart that was discussing the possibility of robbing a Pike County bank.

Chapter Seven

Susan was very upset at learning that Kathy was pregnant, her friends say, and she cried bitterly over Mark's long stay in Connecticut during the winter of 1987. The news that Mark was about to be a father again had come just at the start of their love affair, at a time when Susan was fantasizing about asking Mark to leave his wife and marry her, during a period when Mark needed her to testify in the upcoming trial against Cat Eyes Lockhart.

Carmella vividly recalls Susan's sobbing as she called Mark a cheapskate and Kathy a slut when she and Bo and Carmella stopped at a Wendy's drive-thru to get a snack before their ride back home. Mark had told her he was going to be gone for two weeks, to stay with Kathy, Danielle, and the newborn child in Connecticut over the Christmas season. Susan had given him an expensive jogging suit that day, a Christmas gift it had taken her weeks to settle upon, but Mark had had nothing for her, not even a box of candy or a card to wish her a happy holiday.

"That woman's pregnant again!" Susan had yelped as she gulped down Pepsi and fries in the Wendy's lot.

"You crazy fool! He's married! You're just going to get in trouble," Carmella told her.

"No. He loves me. He's just stuck with her 'cause her parents are rich. He told me they were worth nine million dollars. Hey, Mel, do I look all right? My hair's not messed up, is it?"

"What in the world do you see in him? He's just using you," Bo interrupted, angry at seeing his sister so upset. "I just don't see what's so great about him, Suzie. The guy looks like Barney Fife!"

"Well, you're not so damn great-looking yourself, Bo! He's leaving her anyway; he wants to be with me. He told me so just the other day."

"Are you sure he's going to leave that woman, Suzie?" Carmella asked.

"Well, we've been to a motel all day, and he's talking about leaving her, but he'll lose everything he's got if he leaves her right now."

"Well, if he loved you, he wouldn't be going off with her for so long."

"He does love me! But with that bitch pregnant again . . ." Susan burst into tears. "Oh, Mel, how can he do me that way? What am I gonna do?" she cried.

"Lord have mercy, Suzie, don't you see that he's using you? Just for a good time!"

"He told me he loved me. He said he was going to marry me, and now he's changed his mind!"

"You're crazy for talking to him, Suzie."

"I'll go to that woman and tell that slut that I'm pregnant too. I'll tell her that my baby means something!"

"But you're not pregnant, are you, Suzie?" Bo interrupted.

"No, but . . . well, I might be. Who knows? I might get pregnant any time. God, he's so sexy!"

In mid 1988, Putnam had become adept at balancing his domestic life and his affair with Susan, keeping her hopeful that he would leave his wife while maintaining the appearance of being a family man. As long as he kept Susan Smith in his pocket, Putnam thought, he was sure to make a name for himself in the FBI. After all, here he was, a rookie agent, being credited with putting an end to a bank robbery problem that had plagued the area for almost a year. He'd captured Cat Eyes Lockhart, and now he was after MacArthur Lockhart.

With his career at stake, Mark made certain that Susan's sexual needs were being met, and their affair heated up, Susan giving Shelby all the intimate details of their love life. Mark was spending nights with her at his house now, whenever Kathy was up north, and Susan bragged about his body, telling Shelby how sexy he looked walking around his house in skimpy jogging shorts and cut off T-shirts. She was just wild about him and even wore his clothes when she stayed over with him. She'd brought an olive green pair of his shorts home once.

Whenever Susan was alone with Shelby, she

would perpetually dwell upon Mark's bedroom practices, bragging about how well-equipped he was, claiming that he could have multiple orgasms and that the two of them had sex for hours on end. She said he liked her to be on top, that he liked oral sex, that he was a good kisser, that he was strong and could pick her up and put her into all kinds of different positions she had never even heard of before. In short, Susan described Mark as a superman in bed.

Early in the summer of 1988, Susan informed Putnam about the bank robbery that Mac Lockhart was planning. She also told people close to her that Mark wanted her to take a more active role in "setting up" the crime. Putnam, meanwhile, was figuring if he could successfully wrap up another bank robbery case, he would be able to persuade the FBI to relocate him.

At his bidding, Susan Smith was now pushing three men into pulling off a bank robbery in Phelps, Kentucky. In fact, on many occasions she took the youngest of the three, twenty-four-year-old Paul Frazier, over to the Peter Creek branch of the First National Bank of Pikeville in Phelps at about five-thirty in the morning. While he scouted out the escape route, she waited in her vehicle, parked inside the carwash next door. She offered to be the driver if Frazier needed one, and repeatedly told him that a bank robbery was "easy money."

Susan's prodding went on daily for a period of weeks before the first robbery attempt was actually pulled off. She especially had to work on young Frazier, who was leery of the venture. In the middle of June, Frazier, MacArthur Lockhart, and Pete Blankenship set out to rob the bank, but Frazier backed down and they headed back to Vulcan, where Susan was pacing the floor, knowing that Mark and the Kentucky State Police were waiting in one of the vacant lots near the Phelps bank.

Family members say Susan Smith was in on that unsuccessful caper, having been told by Mark Putnam to "get them to the bank, I don't care how. Give them guns, give them whatever they need." Susan was assured by Putnam that she would be removed from the scene once the robbery had started and law enforcement had arrived. Allegedly Putnam and the Kentucky State Police staked out the Phelps bank for three days, during which time Susan drove Frazier and the others there but couldn't get them to pull off the job.

While all this was going on, Putnam was calling Susan at home constantly, and to keep Kenneth at bay, they devised a system. Whenever Kenneth answered the phone, Mark would hang up. Susan would then call him back from another location or she'd ask Kenneth to go to the store for her so she could have some privacy. Whenever Bo picked up the phone, he had instructions to answer yeah instead of hello if it was safe to ask for Susan.

Sometimes, when Putnam hung up on him, Kenneth turned to Susan and said, "It's your boyfriend calling," and Susan always denied it.

Then she would wait until he was far enough down the road before she returned Mark's call, Bo standing by the living-room window to watch for Kenneth while she wooed Putnam. The phone on the bar in Susan's kitchen had a cord long enough to allow it to be carried all over the house, and there was another phone in her bedroom. Kenneth sometimes picked up that one, trying to listen in on her conversations.

"When Kenneth knew it was Putnam on the phone," Bo remembers, "he would get right up beside her, trying to listen, and sometimes he hung the phone up on her."

By now, Susan was refusing to have sex with Kenneth, and he was sure her brothers and sisters were lying to him, covering up her affair. Although he had no proof, Kenneth was determined to get revenge. Yet, despite the increasingly tense situation at home, Susan was spending more and more time in Pikeville.

It was during the planning stages of the Phelps bank robbery, that Kathy Daniels started making regular trips over to Pikeville with Bo and Susan. Sometimes the two young women went there by themselves; Susan was now driving a Dodge Diplomat, a beige car just like Mark's which she purchased with part of her FBI-informant money. On these trips, Susan repeatedly told her new sister-in-law that she had no feeling left for Kenneth. She loved Mark, she said, and she knew Kenneth was "jealous as hell" over it but didn't care. She'd insist that "Mark-ee-poo" would eventually marry her.

Kathy remembers Susan as always being in a big rush when she came over the Vulcan bridge to pick her up. She said they'd usually stop at a little place called First Choice Market, in a town called Kimper about midway between Freeburn and Pikeville, and Susan would call Mark from the pay phone there. There are no pay phones in Freeburn.

Kathy got a good look at Putnam once or twice, even though he did his best to hide himself from her, slouching down behind the steering wheel and wearing dark glasses.

"He didn't want me to see his face, and Susan was afraid for me to see him," Kathy stated. "I knew he was FBI. And he was good-looking."

Kathy claims "Susan fell all over herself" to please Mark, trying to "talk proud, not like a hillbilly" whenever she got near him. When Kathy later became pregnant by Bo, she said Susan asked her to name the baby Mark if it was a boy, arguing and pleading with her sister-in-law and telling her what a perfect name Mark would be.

"I remember one time, we stopped at First Choice, so she could use the pay phone to call Mark. I gave her a quarter and she came back with a whole handful of quarters. It was like she'd hit the jackpot in Las Vegas, you know; the phone had given her all this change and she was laughing about it, and said she couldn't wait to tell her Mark-ee-poo! But he wasn't in when she'd called and had no idea we were on our way over there. I told her we should turn back, but

Susan just couldn't stay away from him."

Since Susan had no appointment with Mark, she was nervous when she got to Pikeville on that particular day. Putnam still wasn't in his office when she called again from a pay phone outside the courthouse and spoke to his partner, Ron Poole. Usually Kathy went shopping while Susan spent time with Mark, but it was late by the time they arrived that day and the stores in downtown Pikeville were closed, so Kathy went into the federal building with Susan to wait for Mark. Susan's gun set off the metal detector as they walked through the front entranceway of the federal building and she just giggled, but Kathy was afraid they'd get into trouble.

"Don't worry about it," Susan assured her. "Mark knows I pack a gun!" After her initial upset, Kathy figured it must have been a regular occurrence, since no one ever came out and said anything to Susan.

"I saw a man in there and Susan said it was Ron Poole. I just sat by the stairs," Kathy recalls. "After she got through talking with Ron, then she went into the marshal's office. His name was Don [Don Lafferty]. He was an older guy. I heard her talking about Mark, how sexy he was, and then they started laughing, I didn't ask about what."

Susan never did see Mark on that occasion. It was a wasted trip, but she didn't seem to mind. In fact, Kathy got the impression that she was happy just being around Mark's co-workers, that she was trying to become a part of his office. Susan wanted her sister-in-law to believe that she was a necessary part of the FBI's daily operations. She even lied to Kathy about working with Ron Poole on a drug-trafficking case.

Finally, on July 14, 1988, the Phelps bank robbery was pulled off. On that day Mac Lockhart, Pete Blankenship, and Paul Frazier entered the Peter Creek branch of the First National Bank of Pikeville, yelling and waving their firearms.

Lockhart, carrying a sawed-off shotgun, kept the employees at bay while the money was being taken out of the vault by Blankenship and Frazier. The three men got away in a yellow Oldsmobile Omega, later identified as a vehicle stolen from a parking lot in Freeburn. Almost immediately after the robbery occurred, the car was located by State Policemen. Three pairs of brown work gloves were found inside it. Police brought in search dogs and tracked the robbers from the car back to Vulcan, where they lost them because of diesel fuel on the railroad tracks. Putnam and Poole were both on the scene, questioning people in and around Freeburn, trying to locate the men. Susan was conducting her own search, asking people in Vulcan where Mac and the others went.

Pete Blankenship was soon found, hiding behind his house up on a mountain near the bank. A fifty-nine-year-old man with a sixth-grade education, he was holding a red bag containing thirty-two thousand, six hundred sixteen dollars, including some twenty-dollar bills that were part of the bait money. Once caught, Blankenship admitted to police that Paul Frazier and MacArthur Lockhart were the two who helped him rob the bank. He offered this information after being read his rights and was told that he would receive a lighter sentence if he "rolled over" on his partners. In return for his cooperation, he later was sentenced to three years of supervised release.

Lockhart and Frazier were subsequently arrested and charged with bank robbery, but neither admitted to committing the crime. Both men were later identified by an eyewitness who'd seen them in the yellow Oldsmobile, and both were recognizable on the bank's videotape of the robbery.

Paul Frazier told his attorney, Larry Webster, that he'd guessed Susan Smith was an informant but he'd pulled the robbery off anyway. When asked why he would do such a thing, Frazier confessed that he was "kind of in love with Susan." He said he would go to her house and give her information to try to win her affections. In exchange, Susan gave him drugs and one of her guns, a .38 Smith & Wesson.

Ronald Gene Poole, who had been a Special Agent in the FBI for eight and a half years, testified at the Phelps bank robbery trial, held in November, 1988, that three white men had entered the bank, wearing pantyhose over their heads and carrying pistols and sawed-off shotguns.

Poole was able to recall the exact date and time the crime occurred. He also told the court that there were no customers in the bank, and no shots were fired during the robbery.

When it came time for the three men to be sentenced, the judge was hard on MacArthur Lockhart because he'd made no attempt to return any of his part of the stolen money, even though FBI agents had been told by "reliable sources" that he'd hidden his share and that members of Mac's family had access to it.

Indeed, Susan was the FBI's chief source. She'd told Mark that she'd gone on a shopping spree in Williamson, West Virginia, with Mac's wife, Geraldine, soon after the heist. Geraldine had told her that Mac had hidden seven thousand dollars under a rug in their backyard, and Susan had even gotten someone to wade across the Tug River to try to recover the loot. That person, who was not identified, had been spotted by Mac's children, however, and had turned back before getting near the property.

Before he was sentenced, Mac Lockhart told the judge he didn't know what had happened to his share of the stolen money, but Ron Poole was on hand to testify that Lockhart was lying. Because Lockhart was considered the ring leader in the robbery and would not return any of the money taken, he was sentenced to serve a hundred and thirty months in federal prison.

Frazier's attorney appeared before the judge and pleaded for mercy, citing the fact that Frazier had turned over nine thousand dollars of the stolen money to Special Agent Poole as a part of his plea bargain. Webster also stated that Frazier's original role in the bank robbery had been to drive the getaway car, but at the last minute, Pete Blankenship had threatened to kill him if he didn't go into the bank and help pick up the money. Webster further argued that there was no evidence that Frazier had carried a firearm of any kind during the robbery.

Because Frazier had no prior record and seemed to have been coerced by the other two men, his attorney asked the court to give him a lighter sentence to be served at an institution where he could receive vocational training. This being granted, Paul Frazier was sentenced to serve sixty-three months in federal prison.

With the three men behind bars, Susan Smith had again helped Putnam look like a hero. People familiar with the Phelps bank robbery have called it an instance of entrapment, chiefly in the case of Paul Frazier, who, they say, would not have gotten involved in a bank heist if it hadn't been for Putnam's drive to earn points with the FBI and Susan's need to satisfy him. The FBI often conducts operations characterized as "sting" operations, in which a person is given the "opportunity" to commit a crime; however, entrapment hinges on the object's predisposition to commit a crime. Since Frazier had no criminal record the predisposition issue is really in question. After all, it was Susan Smith, at the suggestion of Mark Putnam, who coaxed and guided Frazier, eventually getting him to drive Blankenship and Lockhart to the Peter Creek branch of the First National Bank of Pikeville in Phelps.

Since Kathy Putnam spent more and more time in Connecticut, Susan often insisted that Mark take her to his house. Susan was laying her life on the line, she reminded him, and he had to make it worthwhile. Putnam put up with her badgering and continued the affair, even though she had become a real nuisance by this time, constantly complaining that she didn't get paid enough for her informant work, insisting on being at Mark's side day and night, and calling him continually.

Of course Mark played it cool. He never let Susan see that she was annoying him. In a few more months, he figured, the whole thing would be over. He would then have the transfer he had already applied for. Meanwhile Susan was completely unaware that Mark intended to leave the area. In fact, she thought she really had it made because it wasn't sex in cheap motels or in his car at empty strip mines anymore. She was spending time in Mark's home in Pikeville, one of the most beautiful places she had ever known.

Although Kathy was gone a good deal of the time, it appears that Mark's neighbors and coworkers never suspected him of being unfaithful. In fact, Putnam had a number of women friends in the Pikeville area.

There was the schoolteacher from the neighboring town of Prestonsburg who'd been seen with him at local fast-food joints. This dark-haired woman later insisted that she and Mark were just friends, refusing to discuss their relationship further.

Then there was a local professional woman who, according to a motel employee and police interviews, Putnam had spent the night with in early June of 1989. Allegedly he had taken her to the same place he had taken Susan a number of times, the Goldenrod Motel.

Finally, there was the secretary to the Letcher County Commonwealth Attorney, Kathy Turner, whose ex-husband, a detective with the Kentucky State Police, had worked closely with Mark Putnam on a case involving an auto theft ring. Ms. Turner was reportedly going to Putnam's house on Saturday mornings to do cleaning work, driving an hour in each direction; and police detectives at the Hazard Post, sixty-five miles from Pikeville, later admitted they were sure something was going on between them.

Still, even with three or four other women in the picture, and with all the rumors floating around about Putnam, most people refused to believe he was involved in extra-marital affairs. Much later, even after Putnam had admitted he'd had an affair with Smith, Burt Hatfield, who knew both parties, blamed Susan, claiming she was responsible for the involvement.

"Susan would have made the move, the come-on, not Mark," Hatfield said. "I really think Mark would have tried to fight it off, but know-

134

ing Susan, she couldn't stand a turn-down. She took it personally if anybody turned her down. She had to feel attractive. She wanted everybody to like her. She wanted everybody to think she was the sexiest thing that ever lived. You know, she always had the attitude that said everybody wants me, everybody wants in my pants. She wanted everyone to think she was one hot lady and she felt she had to prove that."

Throughout his involvement with Susan Smith, Putnam often told Burt Hatfield that his marriage was great and that he loved his wife, who was a fine person. Sometimes he mentioned that he felt badly for his wife because she was having such a hard time adjusting to the area.

But off the record, Kathy Putnam later told a newswoman about one of Mark's indiscretions. She said while he was in Florida on official business, he reunited with one of his college girlfriends. Kathy had been given Mark's number by someone at the Pikeville FBI office, and when she dialed it, a woman answered before Mark got on the phone.

In the meantime, Susan dreamed about the day when she and Mark would be man and wife. He had all the qualities she was looking for in a husband, and she was spending more and more time at his home, while Kathy was hundreds of miles away. He even cooked the meals when she stayed at his house, serving them to her and satisfying her every need in a way she had never dreamed a man would. Certainly Kenneth had never treated her that way. Susan was positive it would be just a matter of time before Mark left Kathy and she became the new Mrs. Putnam.

She had even confided to her sister-in-law Nancy, Roy Smith's wife, that she planned to leave Kenneth, telling her that she and Mark were going to run off together and start a family. By the fall of 1988, Susan was blatant about her love affair with Mark. She had gotten to the point where she didn't care about Kenneth's threats.

"When she started to go over there to Pikeville every day, in 1988, she'd come back up here and say 'I'm in love with him,' " Nancy recalls. "And she'd be saying she was pregnant all the time. This was a year or six months before she actually did get pregnant. Every month she thought she was pregnant, and she always threatened to tell Mark's wife."

Nancy said Susan would use her telephone to call Mark about a bill or about money, and just after the Phelps bank robbery trial, she and her sister-in-law got into a big argument over the whole situation in front of the Pic Pac grocery store in Freeburn.

"You know, Suzie, you've sold yourself," Nancy told her.

"I love him. I don't love Kenneth anymore. Kenneth treats me bad! He's hitting me in front of the kids."

"Well, you don't have to put up with that! You can go up there anytime and get your clothes and your kids and move out. But you just won't stay away from that bastard FBI. You're slutting yourself!"

"Hey, don't you be calling me names! I'm doing things with Mark, working with him on a big drug deal right now!"

"You call that work? Going around ratting on everybody just so you can get some money for a car and clothes! You know, one of these days, someone is gonna kill you if you don't watch out."

"Oh, they can't kill me! As long as I'm working with Mark I've got someone to protect me!"

"Well, someone ought to have your ass beat to death! You just think you're so fucking smart, setting all these people up and selling drugs and not going to get caught. I don't know who in the hell you think you are!"

"Nancy, you can just go to hell!"

"That's right, just keep doing your dope and leaving your kids with nobody to watch 'em 'cause I'm not doing it for you anymore! Just keep on running off with that bastard over there in Pikeville and forget about everybody else."

"Hey, don't you start saying I don't take care of my kids! I'm not giving up my kids! I love my babies!"

"Yeah? You're not a good mother, but you are a damn liar, Suzie!"

Minutes later, Susan came out of the grocery store to find her car tires had been slashed. She was irate because Mark was expecting her the next day, and now she had no transportation.

Beside herself because she had no way to get over to see Mark before his wife returned to Pikeville, Susan chased down Nancy in one of the stores and the two women had it out. Susan beat Nancy pretty badly before Burt Hatfield appeared on the scene. It took two men to get Susan into the cruiser, and even then she tried to kick and scratch her way out of the car.

Chapter Eight

Susan had cut her hair pretty short and was frosting it regularly. Mark liked short hair, so she spent hours each week at the beauty parlors in Freeburn, getting it cut over and over again. She had two hairdressers, her sister Shelby and her neighbor Corry; both women said Susan had become obsessive about her looks, keeping herself blond, thin, and tan, no matter what the cost. Shelby thought it strange that Susan was cutting her hair so often, and she couldn't understand why her sister demanded such a short length. Nonetheless, in the beauty parlor behind her house, Shelby would cut Susan's hair just as close to the neck as she could get it.

"Mark always wanted her to shave her hair off, and I finally told her he sounded like some kind of pervert, trying to imagine he was in bed with a guy," Shelby admitted, "but she just roared laughing when I said that."

Mark claimed that his wife's long hair turned him off, Susan told her sister. He thought it was too prissy. Kathy had cut her hair shoulder length once, but he wanted it even shorter. It was something they always fought over. Susan spent hours telling Shelby about Mark's fights with Kathy, about their house, about their kids, always hinting that Kathy probably knew about her affair with Mark. Putnam had told her his wife had once caught him red-handed, walking out of a motel room at night with a woman in Connecticut. That had happened just after Kathy had given birth to Danielle, and Mark had admitted he and his wife had split up for a while and had gotten back together on the condition that he would never cheat on her again.

Shelby said that Susan talked about Mark continually, even describing the way he ate, always like it was his last meal, swallowing hamburgers whole and piling up his plate at the salad bar when they went to Wendy's or some other fast-food joint. She laughed about the mounds of pasta he dished up when he cooked for her at his home, enough to serve two or three people, and the way he devoured it, like he was in a big hurry. Susan said she would just be getting started when Mark, already having finished his food, would be going for seconds. In her descriptions of Putnam, Susan always made the FBI man sound larger than life.

But what struck Shelby most was the fact that Susan described Putnam as someone who never showed emotion, someone who was unable to reveal his feelings. She came to think of him as a man who was almost inhuman, and she told Susan he was no good for her. To Shelby, Susan was a very passionate person, who needed a man who could express his love for her. She didn't approve of Susan's childlike trust in Mark, but her sister found Mark perfect, and she blabbed on about how wonderful he was, insisting that they were in love, that they always had a good time, and claiming he was "down to earth," just the type of guy she could get along with.

By Thanksgiving of 1988, Susan could no longer stand the bleakness of the Kentucky mountains and she decided she was ready to leave Kenneth. She began to talk openly to her parents about Mark Putnam, insisting that the FBI man was going to marry her. She had convinced herself that he would, and she had no interest in hiding her love affair anymore. Still, she had not yet made provisions for moving out of her house in Vulcan, so she had to live there with Kenneth and her kids while carrying on the affair with Mark.

In her attempt to gain status and self-esteem, Susan did everything she could to let people around Freeburn know she had nabbed herself a good-looking, educated FBI man. Though it put her life in jeopardy to talk about being an FBI informant, she did so gleefully. Whenever she mentioned Mark, her face lit up, and she told family and friends that she was secure, financially and emotionally, as long as he was in the picture. She said he would take care of any problem that might arise, and she began to act as though she were untouchable. She believed she could deal drugs, carry guns, set people up, and all the while collect money from the FBI. For her, it was an ideal arrangement.

However, the Freeburn locals who knew of Susan's involvement with the FBI did not think she was walking on solid ground. They had seen too many people used as FBI informants quickly thrown aside. And many people claimed they'd been offered FBI protection and had never received it. It was an all too familiar story. The law didn't care who they used as long as arrests were made, her friends told Susan. But she refused to hear them. Corry was one of the people who knew about Putnam, and she was truly afraid for Susan's life.

"We were friends, and she was open. She'd tell me things. I knew she was working with the FBI, but she'd tell me not to tell anybody," Corry recalls.

Just after Thanksgiving, Corry said Susan called Mark from her beauty shop, in a frenzy to get through to him. At that point, Corry expressed the fears she had about Susan's highly dangerous situation. There were too many criminals around who would think nothing of killing her friend, the hairdresser believed.

"You're not scared that something might happen to you, Suzie?" Corry asked. "You might get shot, you know."

"I need the money. I'm working with him," Susan maintained.

"But are you really in it for the money? All

you ever do is brag about how good he looks and how good he is in bed and how he looks like Randi Travis!"

"Well, he does look like Randi Travis — a little bit."

"I hope you know what you're doing. I just don't want to get into any trouble over you calling him from here!"

"It's a job, Corry! Nothing's going to happen to you because I made a phone call from here! Besides, I always call collect, it won't be on your bill."

Susan also made calls to her FBI man from Shelby's home, telling her sister about the arrangements she made for her trysts with Mark. By the end of 1988, Susan was in the habit of bringing her outfits over to Shelby's in order to get ready to go to Pikeville. That way Kenneth wouldn't see her all decked out and cause a scene. When Kenneth did give her a hard time, she tried to placate him by turning over some of her FBI monies, but this strategy wound up costing her more than she'd expected. Kenneth began to demand money from her regularly, draining her of any cash she might bring home.

Usually, by the time Susan was ready to make another trip to Pikeville, she was flat broke, and Shelby recalls she would often have to give her sister a few dollars for gas. After she fixed Susan's hair and helped her dress, Shelby would watch Susan, a twinkle in her eye, pull out of the driveway, promising to stop back the next morning with the latest news on Mark.

The next day, however, when Susan returned, she usually had nothing of any significance to report. By this time, she and Mark were no longer working on any cases together, so they just hung around his house and had sex. To Shelby, her conversations with Susan about Mark had become redundant and banal. It was always just more talk of Mark's sexual prowess, more exclamations about his beautiful body. However, when the subject of Kenneth came up, their talks turned into high-pitched screaming matches, with Shelby telling Susan to leave him and Susan complaining about the times Kenneth tried to have sex with her, about how she was forever fighting him off.

Then, just before Christmas of 1988, in the weeks before Mark left for Connecticut to be with his wife and kids, Susan became possessed by the idea of getting pregnant with his child. That was going to be her Christmas present to him. She never told Putnam that she had gone off the pill, and during her most fertile time of the month, she insisted on repeatedly having sex with him.

Before Putnam left town for the holidays, Susan believed that she had succeeded in getting herself pregnant. Though it was too early for her to take a test yet, she was pretty certain of it. She thought a baby would insure that her relationship with Putnam would last. She had no idea of what Mark and Kathy were planning—his transfer from Pikeville. Kathy had been complaining regularly to the FBI about

144

bomb threats and Mark was telling other law enforcement agents that they were receiving threatening phone calls, thereby laying the groundwork for a move.

Just days after Susan's twenty-seventh birthday, in early January of 1989, Mark returned from his trip to Connecticut and she went to spend time at his house. She would later tell Shelby that she ran around topless in his bedroom, wearing only his jogging shorts as she served him breakfast in bed. Mark's brother Tim had called that night to report that their mother had been in an automobile accident, Susan said. With her there, Mark didn't call the hospital to check on Barbara Putnam. Instead, he talked about his mother's alcoholism.

Throughout January of 1989, Susan wholeheartedly believed Mark would soon belong to her. She inspected Kathy's jewelry and peeked into Kathy's closet to check out the outfits hanging in it, all the while surmising that these things would someday belong to her. She was now playing the role of Mark's wife, and as far as she was concerned, he displayed all the signs of a loving, caring husband. It wouldn't be long before they would be living happily ever after, she was sure.

Susan only had one complaint about Mark. He was cheap. In their two years of "courtship," he never bought her anything, though she had given him a heavy gold chain, which she had stolen from her brother Bo, and other gifts. When she spoke to him about it, Mark told her he always turned his paycheck over to Kathy, explaining that she paid the bills and held the purse strings tight. In fact, he had originally suggested they stay at his house as a means of saving money. On most nights, Mark and Susan watched TV in his den, often making love on the floor while MTV blared in the background.

Then one morning after she'd spent the night with Mark, Susan went to Shelby's, saying she'd almost got "caught" at Mark's the night before when a friend of Mark's, a cop, had dropped by. She and Mark had been having sex on the living-room floor, and Mark had told her to hide behind the couch while he went to the door. As he was trying to get rid of his buddy, Susan noticed that her slacks and panties lay out in the middle of the living room. She was laughing silently behind the couch because she was sure Mark's friend had noticed them. Later she made a joke about Mark's pet parrot, which had sat silently in its tiny cage next to her, telling Shelby she thought the bird might just say, "Here she is, over here, behind the couch!"

Unfortunately, Shelby, like everyone else, didn't fully believe Susan's tales about her involvement with Mark. Her sister was always claiming to have great love affairs, when in reality she was making everything up, so even with all the details Susan furnished about Putnam, nobody was certain that she was having an affair with the man; there was no concrete proof. Indeed, no one had even seen Mark Putnam except Tennis Daniels and Kenneth Smith and that was early on, during the Cat Eyes' bank robbery.

Even Susan's brother Bo had his doubts. He had driven her back and forth to Pikeville, and she'd always claimed that she had been at a motel with Putnam, but he had no verification of that. Once he'd started to follow Putnam's car after he dropped Susan off, just to see where they really went, but then he'd lost his nerve. And to further confuse the issue, Susan changed her stories from one day to the next, sometimes claiming she was meeting Putnam on business, at other times saying they had been screwing at a vacant airport or on an empty strip-mine road. No one really took what Susan said too seriously, not even Shelby. The idea that she could be having an affair with an FBI man seemed impossible; it sounded like another one of her imaginary romances. Even when she mentioned places they had gone, telling Shelby that she and Mark had spent the night at the Days Inn or at his house, Shelby figured that Susan was lying.

However, Agent Poole was pretty sure Susan was telling the truth about her affair with Putnam. He told Shelby he'd suspected the two were romantically involved when he'd noticed Susan's car out in the Wendy's lot at about six A.M. one morning. Poole told Shelby he'd seen Susan's car parked in the lot on more than one occasion, usually when Kathy was out of town. However, Poole maintained that Susan could have been out with some other man. There were a lot of rumors about her in Pikeville, he said.

In the meantime, Tennis was out of jail on probation and was living in the back bedroom of Susan's house at Vulcan. Tennis's brief encounters with Mark Putnam and Ron Poole left a bad taste in his mouth, and he constantly reiterated his distrust of the FBI, warning Susan to stay away from the two men. He also cautioned his friends to keep their mouths shut around Susan because she claimed to be working with Putnam. She had told her brother that she was helping to trap members of the McCoy gang, to expose their counterfeit operation.

However, Putnam had refused to allow Susan to work the McCoy case, saying he didn't want her in on it because the operation was too dangerous and she might get hurt. But such risks had not prevented Mark from putting Susan in other life-threatening situations. Actually, Putnam was excluding her in an attempt to phase her out of the program.

Whenever she was at home in Vulcan, Susan talked ceaselessly about the McCoy gang, about pulling off drug busts, about all kinds of criminal activities in the area. Her friends and family had heard just about all they could stand for over a year. It was all getting stale, and that was why when she recounted tales about John P. McCoy, the mastermind of the largest bank robbery in West Virginia history, whose trial was coming up in May of 1989, people around her hardly listened. Much of the information Susan relayed seemed too farfetched to be true.

But in fact, eight or ten bank robberies committed in the area had gone unsolved. Allegedly they had been carried out by the McCoy gang in and around 1987 and 1988. Russell Davis, an accomplice in one of the robberies had been killed, and Susan told friends and family that Putnam and the police were looking for Davis's body in the remote Kentucky hills.

After months of unsuccessful searching, Davis's remains were discovered in February of 1989 on Ford Mountain, a remote hilltop in Pike County. Mark Putnam was on the scene, along with the Kentucky State Police and State Forensic Anthropologist David Wolfe. Those in law enforcement considered the discovery of Davis's body a miracle, because reportedly many officers had told Putnam that the search for the missing informant was like looking for a needle in a haystack. For weeks on end, isolated areas of Pike County had been combed with bulldozers, but the region was so hilly and there were so many ravines, it seemed the police were fighting a no-win battle. In fact, Davis was found on the very day the search was scheduled to be halted.

However, Putnam never told Susan the details of the Russell Davis search. She read about the incident in the *Williamson Daily News* and later questioned Mark without getting much feedback from him. Things had changed a lot since they'd first gotten involved back in 1987. In those days, he would joke with her about all of his cases. For instance, in early 1988, Mark had told Susan about the time they'd found J. P. McCoy hiding in a refrigerator to keep from being arrested.

With McCoy's name back in the papers in 1989, Susan brought his name up to Mark whenever she had the chance; it was her way of trying to stay on the inside track of what was going on in law enforcement. But despite her big talk, her drug habit, and the time she spent with Putnam, no one was sure what Susan was up to.

She was constantly on the phone with Mark and appeared to be in a good mood whenever she returned from Pikeville, but her relationship with Putnam seemed bizarre to Shelby. From what Susan's sister could gather, Putnam was aloof, silent — a loner who puttered around his garage and hid in his home when he wasn't on the "beat." He no longer coached soccer; he no longer attended football games. He seemed indifferent to the world around him. And though his wife had practically abandoned him, he didn't seem to be the least bit serious about Susan. Shelby couldn't figure the situation out, but it didn't sit well with her. She never said a word to Susan about this, because she didn't want to upset her.

Susan already had plenty to be upset about. Her pregnancy plan had backfired in mid January when she'd had a miscarriage after a violent argument with Kenneth. She hadn't told Mark about the pregnancy until she'd been certain, but Putnam had dismissed the issue. Convinced that Susan was still sleeping with Kenneth, he had asserted that Kenneth was the father.

No one besides Mark and Kenneth had known that Susan was pregnant. Shelby first heard of it the day Susan came marching in from a Williamson hospital with a pink form telling her how to care for herself after having a D&C. The FBI later verified that Dr. Song Kim had performed the procedure in January of 1989. Shelby immediately assured Susan that she was more fertile than ever, so Susan again determined to get pregnant by Mark. She was hell bent on it.

Life at home had turned into a living hell for her. She hated going back to Vulcan and facing Kenneth and her children. She wasn't paying much attention to the house anymore; she stayed away from Vulcan as much as possible. But Kenneth, determined to put an end to her affair, was causing all sorts of problems. He wanted Susan back home where she belonged, taking care of the children, and in desperation, he decided to report the matter to Mark's FBI supervisor. He sought the advice of Will T. Scott, a Pikeville attorney and a former circuit judge in Pike County.

Kenneth consulted with Scott at the offices of Stratton, May and Hayes, a law firm based in Pikeville. Scott clearly remembers their conversation because he thought it outlandish. Kenneth told Scott that Susan was sleeping with Mark Putnam, the local FBI man, and he said he was afraid he was going to be "set up" by the

FBI and arrested on a drug charge. He also claimed that Putnam encouraged Susan to carry a gun, that he allowed her to deal drugs, and that he was using Susan to entrap people. Smith wanted to know if any of this was legal.

After patiently listening to Kenneth's tale, Scott gave him a number to call, all the while believing that nothing would ever come of it.

"I thought he was strung out. I thought he was paranoid at the time, and I suspected maybe he was in trouble," Scott recalls. "I just couldn't believe him. It was so preposterous that an FBI agent would be doing this, I just didn't give it any attention. I told him to get in touch with the FBI supervisor out of Louisville because I could see he believed he had something to worry about with the local FBI office."

Days later, when Kenneth got up the nerve to call Terry Hulse at the FBI office in Louisville to report the affair, Hulse did not believe Smith was a "credible" source. Hulse later told reporters that he received an "anonymous call" regarding the Putnam-Smith affair.

However, Kenneth claims that for months Hulse denied a call came in from him. The FBI asked him for copies of Susan's phone bills during the missing-person investigation, and he turned over the originals to the FBI through Shelby, only to discover that he was unable to retrieve them or get duplicate copies from the phone company since the phone was not in his name.

Since Kenneth had gotten nowhere with

Susan Daniels (*left*), as a cheerleader in Freeburn, Kentucky. (*Courtesy of Sid and Tracy Daniels*)

Sid and Tracy Daniels, Susan's parents, in their living room. (*Courtesy of Sid and Tracy Daniels*)

Susan's childhood home (*foreground*). Sid and Tracy Daniels stand on the porch of their current home (*center*). (*Photo by Lloyd Kelly Stratton*)

Susan Daniels, 18, in Chicago.
(*Courtesy of Sid and Tracy Daniels*)

Susan Daniels and Kenneth Smith in Louisiana.
(*Courtesy of Kenneth Smith*)

Susan and Kenneth Smith's home in Vulcan, West Virginia.
(*Photo by Lloyd Kelly Stratton*)

Miranda Lynn Smith, Susan's daughter, in the Smith home in Vulcan. (*Courtesy of Kenneth Smith*)

Brady Leon Smith, Susan's son. (*Courtesy of Kenneth Smith*)

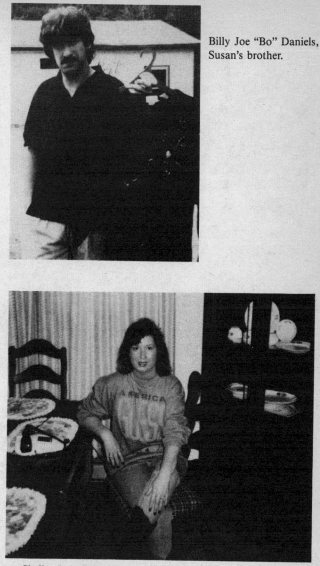

Billy Joe "Bo" Daniels, Susan's brother.

Shelby Jean Ward, Susan's sister, in her Freeburn home. (*Courtesy of Shelby Ward*)

"Cat Eyes" Lockhart and his then wife Sherri Justice. (*Courtesy of Kenneth Smith*)

Mark Putnam proudly holding the ball as captain of the soccer team at Pomfret Academy.

Mark Putnam as a senior at Pomfret Academy.

Mark Putnam at the time of his sentencing for the death of Susan Daniels Smith. (*AP/Wideworld*)

Kathy Putnam.

The former home of Mark and Kathy Putnam in Pikeville, Kentucky. (*Photo by Lloyd Kelly Stratton*)

The United States Courthouse in Pikeville, where the FBI offices were located. (*Photo by Lloyd Kelly Stratton*)

Susan Daniels Smith in Shelby Ward's kitchen just days before her brutal slaughter. She was four months pregnant. (*Courtesy of Billy Joe Daniels*)

The Landmark Inn, where Susan spent her final days with Mark Putnam. (*Courtesy of Lloyd Kelly Stratton*)

Dr. David Wolfe, forensic anthropologist with the Kentucky State Medical Examiner's Office, supervised the discovery of the remains of Susan Daniels Smith on Harmon's Branch, a remote hill nine miles outside of Pikeville.

The skeletal remains of
Susan Daniels Smith.

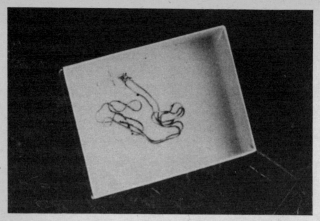

The gold cross and chain that Shelby Ward lent Susan just before her disappearance, found by investigators, near her remains.

A box containing Susan's teeth and fingernails, discovered near her remains.

Susan's jawbone displays two missing teeth. Tests suggest they could have been knocked out at the time of her death.

Kentucky State Police Captain Gary Rose.

Kentucky Commonwealth Attorney John Paul Runyon.

FBI Special Agent Terry O'Connor.

In response to the controversy surrounding the forensic examination of Susan's remains, a Pike County police team was ordered to exhume them from their final resting place in the Elridge Family cemetery. (*Courtesy of the Appalachian News Express*)

The plastic marker on Susan Daniels Smith's grave near Barrenshea Creek in Freeburn, Kentucky. (*Courtesy of Lloyd Kelly Stratton*)

Hulse, he began to try other ways to put an end to Susan's affair. At one point, he called Kathy Putnam and flat out told her that Mark and Susan were sleeping together. "Is that all right with you?" Kenneth asked her, "them going around fucking in motels!" But Kathy just treated the call as harassment, and the next day Mark asked Susan to call her and deny the affair, which she did, telling Kathy that Kenneth was a liar and a drunk.

Susan then went back and blasted Kenneth for making the call to Kathy. She told Kenneth nothing he could do or say would stop her from seeing Mark, but that only made him more determined to try another tactic. He pretended to hire a private investigator in Pikeville, claiming he was having Mark and Susan followed. This shook Susan up, but Mark assured her that Kenneth was lying. Kenneth even had a manilla envelope that bore an investigator's return address mailed to their post-office box in Freeburn in an attempt to frighten Susan, but Mark promised her that Kenneth couldn't lay hands on the kind of money an investigator would charge.

By now, Ron Poole had a fairly good idea of what was going on. Other law enforcement officials had also gotten wind of the Putnam/ Smith affair, and at least one member of the Kentucky State Police, Detective Frank Fleming, had serious doubts about Putnam's moral stability.

Putnam and Fleming had worked closely together from the latter part of October 1987 through December of that year. They had hit it off pretty well at first, although Fleming, a veteran of the force, thought Putnam had a problem understanding how to work the eastern Kentucky area. Putnam was too aggressive, he said. He had trouble tolerating the laid-back ways of the people in the region, which was causing him problems. Fleming wrote Putnam off as being green, too new to the FBI to understand how to get things done, so he used intimidation. His questions were direct and forceful, but he had a lot of learning to do.

"The initial contact I had with Mark Putnam involved the chop shop [auto theft] up in Letcher County. We went up to MacRoberts with a search warrant and then called the FBI in because interstate transportation was involved," Fleming explained. "When Mark took on the case, he and I spent twelve or fourteen hours a day together. At first I liked the guy. Danielle, his daughter, she was his life. He'd come up here and show me pictures of her; he couldn't say enough about her. He talked about their dates on Friday nights. That was one thing I thought was nice."

However, as time went on Putnam became more open with Fleming about the problems he was having adjusting to the area. He was visibly unhappy, Fleming said, and his life seemed strained. He admitted that his mind was wandering away from his wife, and he was carrying around Susan Smith's I.D. picture which he had taken from her FBI file.

"Mark said that he had this informant that he found very attractive and he was really having a hard time remaining faithful to Kathy, because evidently he knew something could happen," Fleming recalls. "He told me he was really wrestling to remain faithful to his wife because this informant was really coming on to him. On toward the end of the chop-shop investigation, he showed me a wallet-sized photo of Susan and she was really a looker. We kidded about it and I said, Kathy's up there, you're alone. You're going to break. But he never came out and said that he had an affair. He talked about it in theory."

Chapter Nine

Regardless of the rumors about Putnam, most of the people he worked with only saw the official side of him and never got any true insight into his personal life. He was deliberately evasive, and knew that no one could prove anything even if some people had their suspicions. As time went on, he made sure that his private life remained a mystery; he spoke less and less to other law enforcement people about what he did when he was off the job.

Corporal Roby Pope of the West Virginia State Police worked with Putnam on the robbery of the Matewan National Bank for a period spanning two years. The two men spent countless hours together trying to find patterns, clues, witnesses, and informants that would lead to the evidence they needed to convict members of the McCoy gang. Pope recalls that Putnam was extremely closemouthed about his personal life, never one to talk about what he did in his spare time or to stick around for a cup of coffee after a meeting.

"We were looking for McCoy in West Virginia, and they were looking for him in Kentucky. Putnam had been involved in the case for over a year, following leads, but nobody would come out and say that John P. McCoy robbed the bank," Pope reminisced. "When Mark was here, he'd be with the Kentucky State Police. We'd have some joint meetings, and he was always business. Afterward, he didn't hang around. He didn't have time to shoot the bull. He was out. He always had some place to go next."

Putnam spoke so little about his family life that once, when Kathy Putnam and her mom were in a serious auto accident in Connecticut, Pope heard through other law enforcement agents that Kathy Putnam had been killed. Pope later found out that Kathy Putnam and her mother were all right, but he learned that from other police officers, not from Putnam. Putnam was just out to solve crimes as far as Pope was concerned, an all work kind of guy who was thoroughly dedicated to "cleaning up" eastern Kentucky. He even told Pope that he was investigating political corruption in Pike County. For one thing, Putnam said that he and Ron Poole were checking out allegations of voter fraud in the area.

Obviously Putnam made sure that Roby Pope never got wind of his involvement with Susan, and he had to be especially careful around him because Susan had revealed she'd worked with Pope on an unofficial basis as an informant. Putnam made sure he didn't bring her name up around Pope, and he never told him that Susan Smith was his informant on the Cat Eyes Lockhart case.

The last time Pope saw Putnam, the FBI man said he was being transferred to Florida. He'd explained that he and his wife were receiving threatening calls; the caller would say the house was being watched and would describe the room his wife was in. "That's why I'm getting an early transfer," Putnam told Pope. "Otherwise I would have been here another three years."

Evidently, Pope didn't think it unusual that Putnam was suddenly being transferred out of Pikeville, although the transfer to Miami was somewhat strange. According to one report, the FBI announced budget cuts somewhere in the fall of 1988 and Putnam, being a rookie agent, was told he would have to stay at the Pikeville office for five years instead of the two years he had originally bargained for. With this crushing news, Kathy reached a breaking point, and Mark would come home every night to find her sobbing uncontrollably. Allegedly the pair came up with a plan to get themselves removed from the Pikeville area, resorting to desperate and unorthodox measures.

Kathy later told an interviewer that she had begun working undercover on a political corruption case, deliberately putting herself at risk, betting on the idea that if she was personally in danger, the FBI would move the family out of Pikeville. Kathy allegedly got the idea from hearing Ron Poole talk about Project Greylord, an assignment in Chicago involving judicial corruption and the mafia. Poole had said that when his life had been threatened he and his family had been moved out of the area.

At any rate, Kathy and Mark told the state police and the FBI that they were receiving continual bomb threats. Kathy even called the Putnams' insurance company to check on their coverage in case of arson or a bombing. She later claimed that when Susan Smith found out about her undercover work, she called her and threatened to have her "set up."

In any event, Kathy continued to report threats to the local police and the FBI. Reportedly, one night when Mark was out of town, a man called and said he was on his way over to kill Kathy. She said she stayed up until dawn, shaking and weeping, alone in her living room, a .357 Magnum aimed at the front door.

In February of 1989 the FBI did move Kathy and her children from eastern Kentucky. It was a covert operation, carried out in the middle of the night. Kathy Putnam never said goodbye to any of her neighbors. She just disappeared. She and the children stayed in Connecticut for two months, until Putnam was transferred to his office of preference—Miami, Florida. Of course, in those months Mark lived alone in Pikeville, and Susan came by regularly.

As she spent more and more time with Mark, Kenneth's anger grew. Not only had Susan thrown him over for another man, now he stood to lose a large part of his welfare support if she left him. Kenneth was further incensed by Susan's saying that if he tried to pull anything, Mark Putnam would set him up on drug charges. Smith's neighbor, Johnny Blankenship, she told him Putnam had come to Freeburn offering five thousand dollars to anyone who would plant cocaine on Kenneth. Frightened and infuriated, Kenneth began hitting Susan in front of the children and other family members. He wanted to humiliate her in every possible way.

"What did you do today?" Kenneth once said in a rage. "Did you go fuck Mark? Did you screw him? Miranda, your mommy's been out screwing today!"

According to Bo, whenever Susan returned from Pikeville, Kenneth walked around the house, muttering under his breath, "Slut, whore," and Susan would scream "Why, you son of a bitch, I wish you'd just leave!" But after a day or so, Kenneth would try to make up with Susan, following her around like a puppy, trying to do her favors, asking if she needed anything from the store and bringing home little gifts for the children.

Then when Susan made another trip to Pikeville, the fighting started all over again, and sometimes Bo would see his sister's lip swollen or her arm bruised. Susan would say, "That bastard over there did it," pointing to Kenneth. Then Bo would get angry and want to fight Kenneth, but Susan wouldn't allow it. "Just forget it. Leave him alone," she'd say.

Despite the anguish she had to put up with in

Freeburn, Susan was seeing more of Mark, having constant sex, determined to get pregnant. She and Mark had the house all to themselves for over two months, and she believed that he and Kathy had agreed to a trial separation. Mark only told her that Kathy had gone back to Connecticut for a while. He didn't inform her that he'd be transferring until much later.

It was at the end of February, within a month of her miscarriage, that Susan became pregnant again. She did not tell Putnam about it at first. Instinct told her to wait. She began having cravings for tuna fish and grapes, she woke up every day with morning sickness, but she couldn't have been more pleased. She knew she had to get out of the Vulcan house. Unwilling to chance Kenneth's interfering with her pregnancy, she planned to move in with Shelby temporarily.

So while Mark was busy making moving and storage arrangements, Susan's thoughts were on when to tell Mark about the baby and where she could live so she could bring it to term in peace. Shelby's would be a fine interim stop, but Susan knew she had to get out of the Freeburn area. She felt sure that Putnam would put her under the federal witness protection program, although he had made no promises to her yet. Convinced of this, she figured she'd wind up living somewhere near him in Florida, she even told Shelby and Kenneth about how the witness protection program worked, claiming that she was about to be removed from the area.

"Before she moved out, things were beginning

to change at home. She wasn't cooking like she usually did. She wasn't doing anything around the house. She didn't spend time with the children," Kenneth recalls. "Her mind was somewhere else. And she began talking about witness protection, claiming that she would just disappear one day. She told me she'd be in a place where no one could find her."

In reaction to her claims, Kenneth threatened to go to Pikeville and harm Putnam. Susan relayed the information to Mark, who then threatened to have Kenneth "set up" on a drug-trafficking charge. In response, Kenneth told Susan that he had pictures of her and Mark entering and leaving Pikeville motels. He said he'd show them to Kathy Putnam. He also threatened to show copies of their phone bill to the FBI. Susan took as many phone bills as she could find and promptly shredded them, throwing them, like confetti, into the Tug River.

In his determination to expose Mark Putnam and hang on to Susan, Kenneth began to tape his conversations with Susan, intending to bring the tapes to the authorities if need be. He wired a mini tape recorder to his body and had Susan openly admit to the affair with Putnam. In these recorded conversations, she talked openly about her love affair, her drug dealings, and about the money she received from the FBI for her "work," admitting that all along she and Mark had been making love in various motel rooms and billing everything to the FBI.

Kenneth taped much of what Susan said in the

weeks before she left the Vulcan house to move in with Shelby, and he brought the tapes to Kelsey Friend, Jr., for safekeeping in mid March. He told Friend that if anything ever happened to him, the tapes would prove he'd been wise to some of the "goings-on" inside the FBI. Friend refused to listen to the tapes, but his records show that he did, in fact, log them into his office.

In the first tape-recorded conversation, Kenneth targeted Mark Putnam's knowledge of Susan's drug dealings and Putnam's willingness to support her criminal behavior.

"Would you let me finish, okay? If I work with them, they'll protect me! If I don't work with them, you think they'll protect me? Shit, no!" Susan was speaking, her children crying in the background.

"I just don't want anybody trying to blow my ass up! Here you are dealing drugs, and that's supposed to be just fine!" Kenneth was responding.

"I told Mark, I've got bills. He said if I don't have enough money, my hand to God, he said to deal—wide open! He said for me to deal! He said if I get busted in some way, he'll get me out of it."

"He said he's going to help you out if you get busted? He knows about you dealing?"

"I told him I do coke. I told him I deal, just like that. And I asked, if I got busted—bad, you know—say my house gets raided, are you guys going to help me out? And Ron and Mark both said they'd do it. We won't let you go to jail, they said."

163

On another tape-recorded conversation, Susan talked to Kenneth about Putnam's bedroom practices.

"So you're going to motels with him?"

"Yes."

"How long have you all been going to motels, Susan?"

"That's none of your business."

"I know but—"

"Me and Mark's been dating about a year and a half."

"So . . . I knew it all along, and you've been denying it!"

"Yep."

"Have you been going to his house?"

"That is none of your business. That is nothing to you, and if you go calling and telling Kathy, she won't believe you. She doesn't want you calling her, so what are you going to do now? Go to her house and try to make her believe you? It's none of your business anyway."

"He told you he loved you?"

"Yes he did."

Later in the recorded conversation, when Kenneth brought the issue of marriage and pregnancy up, Susan pretended that she did not want to have any serious involvement with Putnam or any other man.

"What would you have done if you had come up pregnant? Would you have had his baby?"

"Well, Kenneth, yes, I guess, if I didn't have the money to have an abortion. I told him I already have two kids. I don't want any more. They're too

164

hard to take care of, and I don't want any kids to take Brady and Miranda's place. I just want Brady and Miranda."

"What if he made you stay pregnant and have his baby?"

"I wouldn't want to stay pregnant. I'd just see if I could get the money to have an abortion."

"Well, you don't care anything about me or the kids anymore, so I don't see why you don't just have a kid with him!"

"I love my kids and I'm going to raise my kids!"

Finally Kenneth tossed in the idea that Kathy might find out about the affair.

"Hey, what are you going to do if Kathy ever does find out?"

"She knows we go to a motel to talk. She knows we go there to work together. She doesn't know we're going out."

"She knows you're in there four or five hours?"

"She knows people stay in there a long time. She loves Mark. She trusts him. She's been with him five years."

"And you can handle that?"

"Yes, 'cause I don't want to get married again. I don't want any steady relationships anymore."

"So you can handle you and Mark just having sex in a motel?"

"No, Kenneth. It's not just sex. It's other things. We're real good friends. . . . I'm sorry I fell in love with somebody, Kenneth. I'm sorry."

"So you fell in love with a married man?"

"Yeah. My God, I wish he wasn't married, but

he is, and I'm not going to quit him just because he's married. I'm not going to do it, 'cause I can't!"

"You love him that much?"

"Yes, I do."

"And he loves you that much too?"

"I don't know, Kenneth. I don't know how much he loves me. He said he loves me. I didn't ask him how much."

"Who pays for the motel when you go there? The FBI?"

"That's none of your business! I don't know who does. I stay in the car. I don't really want to talk about it anymore. Why are you asking me all these questions?"

"And Kathy believes you all are working?"

"We are working together—as a team!"

"Yeah, as a team, in motel rooms!"

Just days after Susan moved in with her sister, in late March, Mark told Susan about his transfer. She was stunned, all the more so because she was now sure she was pregnant.

Desperate to keep Mark by her side before he left, Susan called him from Shelby's every day to cry about all the problems she was having. She used any excuse to call and beg him for help. And she needed it. Kenneth had burned all of her new outfits and all of her high-heeled shoes. Shelby had had to take Susan over to Williamson and charge the clothes she bought her on a credit card because Susan had arrived at her sister's with only

166

the clothes on her back. Now Susan owed Shelby money. She had supplemented her wardrobe with yard-sale clothing and was borrowing some of Shelby's things, but she had no decent underwear anymore. Everything is gone, she told Putnam. Kenneth had even tossed all of her makeup and jewelry into the fire, and he had burned her purse, which contained her social security card and her birth certificate. She would have to reapply for these or she might lose most of her welfare money.

But it didn't faze Mark that Susan was left with nothing. All he cared about was what he wanted—to be out of Pikeville. It meant little to him when Susan said Kenneth would no longer allow her to see her kids, that her brother-in-law, Ike, was threatening to throw her out of his house if she kept up her involvement with the FBI.

Susan's life was in chaos. In late March, she drove to Pikeville to tell Mark about the pregnancy. The news was not welcome, certainly not when Putnam was making final preparations to leave town. At first, he was nonchalant about Susan's baby, denying that he was the father. Then she made another trip to see him. This time she insisted that Mark help her with the child. He told her he was about to complete his transfer, but acted concerned, promising to take good care of Susan, even after he moved away.

Chapter Ten

Mark and Susan said their goodbyes at the Super America gas station on the South Mayo Trail in Pikeville. He used his government credit card to fill her gas tank up, and Susan later told Shelby that she saw a tear in his eye as he pulled away, a U-Haul hooked to the back of his car. Perhaps, as Mark looked back, the town seemed unreal to him. Like a cardboard Hollywood set, it stood, hauntingly silent against the backdrop of the Pike County mountains.

Susan drove to Shelby's, in tears, thinking of the good times, back in 1987, when she and Mark walked around some of the local lakes as a couple, holding hands in the moonlight; contrasting his loving behavior back then with the short-tempered and uneasy person she'd waved goodbye to moments before. Her stomach sank as she thought of his present attitude. She was worried, because sometimes he acted like the baby wasn't his, trying to deny everything. In one breath he accused her of sleeping around — with

Ron Poole, Burt Hatfield, Kenneth, and everybody in town — in the next, he told her he loved her and would help her in any way he could. "We'll work something out," he'd said before he drove off. "I'll be back." His bland assurance rang in her ears. But she was afraid she might never see Mark again, and she was hurt because he wouldn't give her any money to help her through the pregnancy.

Putnam was on his way to meet Kathy and the children at the Miami motel where they were staying while waiting to move into their town house. The Putnams had purchased a place near Fort Lauderdale, on Woodgate Place in Sunrise. It was located right on a canal, and with the bright sun and a glimpse of the Atlantic to brighten their days, Mark figured he and Kathy could start their marriage all over again — without having to worry about Susan Smith and her problems. In Florida, he and Kathy would be able to get their lives in order.

But as Mark spent his days adjusting to the fast pace of Miami, Susan just sat around Shelby's house daydreaming, staring out the front door, tears in her eyes. She had not heard anything from Mark for days, and she tried to envision his new life, although his secretiveness about where he would be living and what he would be doing was frustrating. She could no longer get Putnam to divulge any information about his family or his work.

In an attempt to keep tabs on him, Susan called Ron Poole, seeking understanding and sympathy. After calling Poole just about every day to complain about her unhappy circumstances, Susan finally took a trip to Pikeville and insisted that Ron give her the number of Mark's motel in Florida. After some hemming and hawing, Poole gave in, and she wrote the number down on a scrap of yellow paper.

After racing back to Shelby's, Susan stared at the yellow slip of paper with Mark's number on it — area code 703 — and then wrote "Mark loves Susan" and "Susan loves Mark" all around the number while she tried to get up the nerve to dial it.

When Susan finally got through to Mark's motel room, about a half-hour later, Kathy answered the phone. Shelby overheard the conversation. Susan was asking Kathy about Florida. She wanted to know whether Kathy liked it there, and she asked where Mark was. Kathy told Susan that Florida was beautiful, that she was happy there. She said that Mark had just stepped out for a minute but would soon be back. "Well, have Mark call me, Kathy. It's business," Susan told her in a mustered formal tone.

A few minutes later Shelby's phone rang. It was Mark calling from the lobby of the motel. In her initial conversation with him, Susan didn't mention the pregnancy. She just talked about being bored at Shelby's. There was nothing for her to do, she said. Shelby and Ike just sat around and watched TV at night, and during the day they were out working and she was all alone. She told Mark that she might get Shelby to take her to see him, but Putnam put her off, assuring her that he would soon be back in Pikeville to wrap up the "chop-shop" case, involving a string of tractor trailer thefts.

Shelby recalls that Susan and Mark called each other a number of times without Susan ever saying a word about the baby. Shelby couldn't understand that, and whenever her sister was on the phone she would sit behind her, whispering, "Tell him about the baby! Tell him you need support!" But Susan would just motion her sister away, claiming the timing wasn't right.

After another few weeks had gone by, Susan convinced Ron Poole to pick her up in Freeburn and take her to Pikeville for a little excitement, and toward the end of April, 1989, Poole drove Susan to Pikeville for the "Hillbilly Days" celebration.

Hillbilly Days is a half-serious, mostly mock festival. It draws thousands of people from neighboring states, people who come to "dress hillbilly" and to show off their "hillbilly 'mobiles" in the streets of downtown Pikeville. It's quite a show, with a backdrop of mountain music, clogging, and square dancing, and people parading in overalls and straw hats, their front teeth painted black, smoking corncob pipes.

In recent times Hillbilly Days has become a commercial success. Pikeville vendors and businesses pull in thousands of dollars during the four-day event, and many craftspeople and artists demonstrate their work on the city streets, trying to sell their wares to the curious passers-by. It's the one time of the year that business flourishes because people from the area dig into their pockets to spend whatever they might have. Ron Poole took Susan around to the booths lining the streets, buying fried apple pies, hot dogs, and pizza. They both ate a lot, especially Susan, since she was past the morning-sickness stage and was now hungry all the time.

Still, the trip to Pikeville did not cheer her up. She complained to Ron about Mark as they strolled from one crafts exhibit to another. Not even the lively music or dancing could divert her, so Ron, in an effort to appease Susan, took her into Watson's Department Store and bought her a new outfit, which she quickly changed into, wearing the new clothing for the remainder of their day together in Pikeville. She had picked out a red top and a matching pair of red- and white-striped shorts, and Poole even bought her a pair of white high heels to complete the look. Susan later told Shelby that Ron had wanted her to get red shoes, but she had insisted on the white pair, thinking the red high heels would make her look trampy.

Since Mark had left town, Susan's whole demeanor had changed. She wasn't as outgoing, wasn't as much fun to be around. She didn't want to socialize anymore, and she didn't want to be seen in outfits that might attract other men. She wanted Mark to marry her, she told Poole that day in April. She wanted to be a respectable woman.

Poole tried to divert her. He talked about other

subjects. In fact, he never said a word about Mark that day. Whenever Susan brought Putnam's name up, Ron pretended he didn't hear her and quickly pointed to one of the Hillbilly exhibits. That night, he left Susan at the Freeburn Post Office across from Shelby's house. This had become their meeting place, since Susan had to hide her involvement with the FBI from Ike. She couldn't let her brother-in-law see her in Ron's silver Blazer. Ike, and everybody else in Freeburn, knew Poole's car.

As soon as she walked through the door of her sister's home, Susan showed off the outfit Ron had bought her; then tears came to her eyes when she discovered that Mark still hadn't called. She took the outfit off, handed Shelby the red top as a gift, and went back to staring out the front door, becoming more withdrawn and introverted than ever. She wouldn't even talk about Mark or his wife anymore. Shelby was confronted with an altogether different person now. Susan hardly said a word to anyone. It was as if she put herself on ice. She was no longer the adrenaline-driven young woman everyone knew and loved.

In an effort to pull her sister out of the slump, Shelby would say, "Susan, why don't you get out for a while — go for a walk or something — or we'll go out riding around?" But each time Shelby suggested an outing, Susan refused, saying she needed to be near the telephone in case Mark called. She retreated to the TV set and would sob uncontrollably whenever a police show came on, especially *Miami Vice*, which she watched in great pain, thinking of the days she'd spent with Mark on drug stings, wondering what stings he was pulling off in Miami, and hoping each time the phone rang, it would be Mark on the line, calling to say he was going to arrange to move her to Florida.

By the middle of May Susan was getting desperate about her situation. She was afraid to talk to Mark about the baby, but Shelby insisted that she approach the subject of her pregnancy over the phone with Putnam. Susan was starting to show now, being almost four months along, and Shelby was exasperated by her sister's timidity. She finally got Susan to confront Mark on the telephone. Shelby heard Susan's part of the conversation, and Susan filled her in on Mark's responses after hanging up. Shelby said their talk started off friendly enough, but the discussion turned nasty when Susan started making demands.

"Kathy told me she liked it down there and you all are getting along good and she's happy," Susan remarked.

"Yeah. It's beautiful down here. How's everything back up there?"

"Well, just fine. I miss you a lot. You and Kathy been having any sex lately?"

"No, Susan. I've been too tired to bother with her. I'm getting settled into the new office and all. I've had so much work to do, I don't have time for anything else."

"Yeah, I bet! Why haven't you been calling me since you've been down there? I've left messages at your office. Haven't you been getting them?"

"Well, what it is, Susan, I'm new and I'm out a lot and they don't know how to find me, so I haven't been getting all of my messages. And in this office here, I don't have my own private office, they have everyone in one room, like in stalls, you know, so you have to get your calls put through an operator. It's hard for me to call you from there."

"Well, have you all found a place to live yet?"

"Yeah, we've moved into a town house near Fort Lauderdale."

"A town house!"

"Yeah."

"Well, I hope you all are enjoying yourselves! And you better enjoy it while you can, because when I'm through with you, there won't be any town house, I can tell you that!"

"What are you talking about, Susan?"

"You're going to support this baby, that's what I'm talking about!"

"You don't even know if I'm the father, do you?"

"Damn straight I do! It's your baby, Mark, and I want some child support! I can't do this on my own!"

"Look, we'll talk about it when I get back up there, okay?"

"You are going to give me money for this baby, Mark, or I'll get Shelby to bring me down there and we can fight it out in front of Kathy!"

"We'll get everything straightened out as soon as I get to town, Susan. Just trust me on this."

After Susan hung up, she just sat, real quiet, and after a while, as she told Shelby what Mark said, she started to cry.

"I feel like I'm going to die," she said.

"What in the world is wrong with you, girl?" Shelby asked.

"I don't know. Kenneth won't let me see my two kids, and now I'm going to have this one and Mark won't do anything for me."

Shelby was so angry about Susan's situation she was tempted to offer to drive her down to see Putnam. She'd considered doing that many times, to get the situation with Mark resolved, because life in Freeburn was much more difficult with Susan in the house. Ike suspected that the FBI was poking into his business, and Kenneth constantly circled the house, checking up on Susan's whereabouts, always ready to start a fight, always trying to make trouble.

Most days, Kenneth would pull up out front. He'd have the kids in the car and he'd ask Susan to come out and talk, but she would refuse because she didn't want to fight in front of the children. And Susan had good reason to fear Kenneth. Shelby remembers one hot spring day in early May, when she encouraged Susan to go out to Kenneth's car and deal with him for Miranda and Brady's sake, Susan wound up bruised and threatened.

As soon as Susan had gotten into Kenneth's car, they'd started arguing bitterly. In front of Miranda and Brady, Kenneth accused her of having men visit her, of being a drug addict and a whore. Susan cursed him for spying on her and for making up lies in front of the kids, of trying to turn them against her.

Enraged, Kenneth drove off with Susan and the kids, and as they continued to argue, he opened the passenger door of the car and shoved Susan out into a ditch. She was hysterical when she called Shelby from a neighbor's, and a short time later, covered with mud, she came back to Shelby's, her right leg bruised. Susan told her sister that Kenneth had a gun and he'd threatened to take her over to the railroad tracks in Vulcan and blow her brains out. With a trembling voice, she said Kenneth had practically run over her after he'd pushed her out of the car.

On May 7, 1989, Susan Smith filed a warrant of arrest charging Kenneth Smith with terroristic threatening. She stated in her complaint that Kenneth had threatened to shoot her, that he'd directed obscenities at her, and that he'd attempted to run her over with his car. She also called Ron Poole and told him about the incident with Kenneth, and she begged Poole to help her get out of Freeburn. Poole was polite but noncommittal.

By the end of May, Susan was convinced that Mark was trying to weasel out on her. She didn't want to face that ugly reality, but she kept remembering an incident that occurred before he left town, when he had driven her around Fishtrap Dam over by Pikeville and had acted like a crazy man when she'd brought up the subject of her pregnancy. Putnam had tried to push Susan out of the car, and Susan now realized that he might have been trying to destroy their child.

Ultimately Susan broke down and told Shelby about that frightening scene with Mark.

"When I asked him for monthly child support, he started banging his hand on the steering wheel. He was saying, 'I cannot do that! Any check I write will be traced! Kathy's got my accounts tied up!' And he was screaming, having a fit," Susan reported.

"Susan, if you don't watch, he sounds like a crazy man, and he's going to hurt you in some way, maybe even kill you! The guy's nuts!" Shelby told her.

"No, Shelb. You worry too much. Mark could never hurt me or do anything like that. He's not that type of person."

"Yeah?"

"Wait until you see how pretty this baby is going to be! It's going to be a little FBI baby!"

"Yeah, maybe it'll have FBI branded on its ass!" Shelby sneered.

Shelby knew Susan had no idea of the danger she was in. Susan had always made things work in her favor, even if she didn't have good sense, but this was a whole different matter. She was dealing with an FBI man, and he was sly, much too sly for her. Shelby began to worry about Susan's pressuring Mark, and in her fear, she told their parents what was going on.

"I told her to stay away from the FBI. I said that man wasn't going to lose his job over her,"

Sid Daniels later declared. "But she just wouldn't listen. I told her to take her baby and raise it herself, to forget about Mark Putnam. She wasn't going to get him to leave his wife. Anyone with any sense would have realized that."

But rather than heed her father's advice, Susan retreated further into her drug habit. Shelby feared that she was harming her unborn child, and the two sisters got into constant arguments about that, and about Shelby's attempts to get Susan off drugs. Susan only wanted to drown her sorrow over Mark.

However, unknown to her, Putnam returned to Pikeville in May of 1989. He stayed at the Landmark Inn on May 23 and 24, using his American Express card to pay for the two nights. Ron Poole also checked into the Landmark Inn for those two days. And Putnam left town without contacting Susan.

Susan continued to call his office in Florida, however. Mark could not ignore all of her calls, so he started calling her back from pay phones to learn the status of her "supposed" pregnancy.

One day when he called her, Susan told Shelby she would take the call upstairs. She said she had a lot of things to tell Mark that would be best said in private.

"Boy, I really let him have it this time!" she claimed when she came downstairs. "I told him he was going to have to give me some child support. Then he said he'd pay for an abortion, but I told him no, I'm keeping the child!"

According to her sister, Susan now thought she

had scared Mark, had him convinced that if he didn't start paying support, she would get Shelby to drive her to Florida and would appear on Kathy's doorstep with her big belly. Mark had said he couldn't pay her anything. He still contended that he had no money, that Kathy took care of the bills. However, Susan persisted, until Mark told her they'd discuss it when he flew back to Pikeville to settle the chop shop case.

After repeating her conversation with Mark, Susan asked Shelby what Florida looked like. She only knew it from TV, and she couldn't believe the place was really as beautiful as the television shows made it seem. But Shelby described it as a paradise, with palm trees, blue surf, and white sandy beaches—a tropical heaven filled with fruits and flowers and a lot of rich people—and Susan's face lit up when she heard that. Then, after a few minutes, her eyes swelled up, and her smile vanished. She sat tapping her long nails on the kitchen table as she told Shelby, "I'm going right out of my mind. These people sit back in the mountains with their wringer washers out on the porch and dogs and pigs out in the yard, and they walk around spitting chewing tobacco and doing nothing all day. I can't stand it. I want something else out of life. I don't want to have to go on living like this. You know, if they don't put me under witness protection, I'm going to ruin them—ruin them all. I know enough about Mark and all of 'em. I'll tell the FBI. I'll get them all in trouble!"

"Suzie, what do you have on the FBI?" Shelby asked.

"I can't tell you, Shelb, it's too dangerous."

"Oh, tell me, Suzie! I won't say a word to anybody," Shelby prodded.

"No, I'm not going to tell you, because you've got a big mouth, and as it is, I'm in danger. I don't want to put you in danger, too!"

As Susan awaited Mark's arrival for the chop shop trial, Kenneth called her every day and asked her to come up to the Vulcan house to see the kids. Their conversations always ended in arguments, with Kenneth accusing Susan of being a whore and Susan slamming down the phone. Kenneth had reported Susan's illegal income to the welfare office, telling social workers that she was receiving money from two states. As a result Susan's benefits were cut down, as were Kenneth's. Since Susan had no money coming in from the FBI anymore, she only had two hundred forty-nine dollars a month to live on. Finally, she agreed to go to Williamson to sign papers giving Kenneth full custody of both children, so he could continue to draw welfare and support them.

Shelby remembers the day Susan and Kenneth went to Williamson. Mark called many times, and when Shelby finally told him that Susan was with Kenneth, he told her he'd call back later and hung up.

Mark never did get through to Susan that day, and she burst into tears when she discovered she had missed his calls. She even blamed Shelby for not contacting her somehow.

The last week of May, at Kenneth's bidding,

Susan finally agreed to go up to Vulcan and spend a few days with her family to try to make peace. By now, it looked like Mark Putnam was completely out of the picture, and Susan knew she had to come up with some way to change her dire circumstances for the better. She decided to try to make things up with Kenneth. Even though she had gotten a warrant to keep Kenneth away from her, and she still wasn't sure he would not harm her, she had no alternative.

Susan and Kenneth had agreed that she would sleep on the couch and he would sleep in the bedroom with the kids. And while she was at the Vulcan house, Kenneth came up with a plan to get them all out of Freeburn. He called his brother Roger, now living in Seattle, and made arrangements for the four of them to stay with him for a while. Susan decided that she would go to Seattle and get away from it all. She and Kenneth had a long talk about it. They agreed to live together for the children's sake, but they would not sleep together.

She told Kenneth to sell the furniture and get the rest of the kids' clothes boxed up in preparation for the move. They had decided to sell everything, including the car, and to fly to Seattle, taking the bare minimum of clothing and toiletries. Susan had already packed some clothing before she left the Vulcan house and headed back to Shelby's. Kenneth's sister, Irene, had given her some large-sized items that would be good for maternity wear, and that was about all Susan had at Shelby's. She was going back there to pack her things, and to get everything squared away before their move.

She explained to Kenneth that she couldn't leave for a few days. She had to go to Pikeville, she said, to work out the terms of getting paid what the FBI owed her. In addition, she hoped the FBI might put her under witness protection. Then she could have a whole new identity in Seattle. If that were the case, their lives would run much smoother.

But, as soon as he felt sure he had won Susan back, Kenneth harassed her even more frequently at Shelby's, accusing her of sleeping with other men and of getting drunk, continually calling her a slut and an unfit mother. Finally Susan got disgusted and backed out of the plan to go to Seattle. She knew going there with Kenneth would not work out.

Desperate, she had to come up with a new plan. On May 30, 1990, she had Shelby drive her over to the Pike County Health Department, where she had a urine sample tested to prove she was pregnant. She and Shelby then took the positive result slip to Ron Poole at the FBI office. Shelby noticed that Susan had a special knock she used when they got there. By now, the FBI quarters were in a new location, on the fifth floor of the First National Bank of Pikeville, and on the way up in the elevator, Susan filled Shelby in on Ron's FBI work, telling her he had worked undercover for two and a half years in Chicago, had been based in St. Louis for eight months, and had been an agent for over eight years. She said Ron was a nice guy, who didn't look like an FBI agent.

When Poole opened the door, Shelby, who had never seen him, couldn't believe how big he was — agent Poole was over five feet eleven inches and weighed almost three hundred pounds. And his clothing surprised Shelby. It was unkempt. He was involved in some kind of undercover work, Susan said. Poole was wearing his hair long, and Shelby remembers that she couldn't believe he was an FBI agent.

As soon as the two women walked into the office, Susan showed Ron the pregnancy test, proudly saying that the Health Department had told her the baby was due in November. Ron looked at the positive result slip and the various pamphlets Susan had been given, on sensible eating during pregnancy and the special supplemental food program for infant children, and his immediate reaction was, "Hey, this is really good! I'm going to take these down the hall and photostat them and leave copies on Mark's desk so he can find them when he gets back!"

Poole got so worked up about the pregnancy, he left the two women alone with all of the FBI files at their disposal while he disappeared for a few minutes, later telling them never to let anyone know he had done this. After Poole placed copies of the positive pregnancy results in his and Putnam's desks, he asked the women to have a seat.

"This is Mark's baby, Ron. What do you think I should name it? How about Mark if it's a boy or Markella if it's a girl?"

Poole just laughed and winked at Shelby.

"Lord, don't stick the baby with a name like Markella," Shelby teased.

Shelby thought Poole acted as though he knew about the affair, but he didn't come out and admit it. Not even when Susan joked about Mark knocking her up and got Ron and Shelby to laugh about it, going into detail about her sex life and talking about Mark's "equipment" in a way that embarrassed her sister.

Shelby was nervous, but Susan began to describe Mark's house and Ron said he had been there once with his wife for a cookout. He added that he didn't like Kathy Putnam because he'd overheard her and Mark making fun of his weight. He never visited them again. Overall, Shelby found Poole very sympathetic.

Finally, he said Putnam was due back in Pikeville on June 5, and before the two women left, he promised he would get Putnam to straighten everything out then. Police would later confirm that Poole mailed copies of the positive pregnancy result slip and the pamphlets on prenatal care to Putnam at the FBI Miami office.

Then, in a twist of fate, just two days before Putnam's return to Pikeville, Susan got into a fight with Sherri Justice, the ex-girlfriend of Cat Eyes Lockhart. That gave her a real reason to require witness protection, and she felt sure that Mark and Ron would help her get out of the Freeburn area.

After she told Shelby what had happened, she called Ron Poole, who came over the next day to take a picture of Susan's smashed car window. Shelby had taken pictures of Susan's torn, hot pink blouse — it had been ripped to pieces — and she showed them to Poole as soon as he arrived, but kept them to show the police later.

Of course Susan might have been using the Justice fight as a ploy to get out of Freeburn. Indeed, Kenneth Smith contends that she was forever calling the FBI office and claiming that her life was in danger, saying that people in Freeburn were beating her up and throwing rocks through her windows, but none of it was true.

According to Kenneth, on the day of the fight with Sherri, he saw Susan rip her own blouse and take a piece of the broken glass and cut her own leg. He said Susan wanted to make the FBI think she was really roughed up, when in fact she wasn't hurt that badly.

"She wanted them to think she was hurt more than she really was," Kenneth claims, "she was trying to get under witness protection. That's why she cut herself with the glass. I couldn't believe it when I saw that. But she did that all the time. For months, she'd keep a package of bandages in the glove compartment of her car and she'd put that stuff on before she went over to Pikeville. I knew what that was for."

And it wasn't only Kenneth who noticed Susan's desperate attempts to get attention and help. Her brother Bo also contends that Susan often pretended to be in danger, hoping that would get her out of Freeburn.

"One time a truck drove by and knocked one of

the pieces of gravel from the railroad track through the living-room window in Vulcan, and Susan ran and called Mark and said one of the bank robbers had thrown a brick through the window. She had him believing her life was in danger, and she tried to get me to believe her, even though I was there when it happened. I saw that it was just a piece of gravel, but she wouldn't listen to the truth, she wanted me to buy into her story. Really, she just wanted to get under witness protection."

Ploy or no ploy, between the pregnancy test and the Justice beating, Susan got Ron Poole's sympathy and she also got him to swear to contact her the minute Mark arrived in town. By now, she had Poole eating out of her hand. She had cried to him about her financial problems so often that he even agreed to meet her at Druthers, a restaurant in Meta, a town halfway between Freeburn and Pikeville, to give her a little bit of money to help with her prenatal expenses. At that meeting, Ron promised that Mark had already agreed to deal with the pregnancy as soon as he returned to Pikeville. Still, Shelby thought the whole business was strange; Ron Poole was acting more like the father of Susan's child than Mark Putnam.

Chapter Eleven

On Monday, June 5, Mark Putnam made the two-hour drive from the Huntington, West Virginia, airport, taking Highway 23 through Paintsville, Kentucky, and winding swiftly through the mountains in his rented Ford Tempo, the roads slick with rain water. He reached Pikeville in record time, having much business to conduct in preparation for the trial.

It rained all that day, and Susan periodically called Ron at the FBI office to see whether Putnam had arrived. Poole told her Mark was aware that she had had a pregnancy test and the results were positive. He promised he would call the minute Putnam walked through the door.

Susan hadn't laid eyes on Mark since he'd left town in April. She was jittery about what would happen when he saw her, so noticeably pregnant, and she was anxious to get to Pikeville. She hadn't been there since she'd had the pregnancy test done.

At approximately six P.M., Ron Poole telephoned Shelby's and asked to speak to Susan.

"Guess who just walked in?" he told her with a chuckle.

"Who, Mark? Put him on the phone," Susan shrieked.

She was sure Mark would invite her to stay with him at his motel, but much to her dismay, he didn't seem happy to hear her voice. In fact, he rushed her off the phone. During their short conversation, she told him all about the Sherri Justice beating, and he listened but made no comment. He acted as if she were a nonentity, not even paying attention to her story, she later told Shelby. He had work to do on the chop shop case, he claimed, and he was too busy to see her. Before he got off the phone he promised he would call her soon, then hung up before she could protest.

Of course, Susan wasn't satisfied. She wanted to see him right away, and the minute she hung up, she took a shower and put on one of Shelby's brand-new outfits. Shelby tried to talk her out of going to Pikeville, but Susan was determined to see Mark. She asked Shelby to help her fix her hair and put on makeup.

It was nine P.M., still raining, fog covering the mountains with a thick gray shroud, when Susan called Ron Poole at his home just outside Pikeville along John's Creek to tell him that Mark wanted to see her over at the Landmark. Poole advised her to wait until the morning. He argued that the roads were too dangerous, there was no visibility, and it was already late.

But Susan was insistent, telling him to pick her up immediately because Mark wanted her over in Pikeville that night. After some begging and pleading, she finally got Poole to agree to pick her up at the Freeburn Post Office. He would be there by ten-thirty P.M., he said.

Susan and Shelby waited together at the round wooden kitchen table, sitting in their chairs, their eyes flashing over to the big clock on the paneled wall, their backs stiffening. Susan kept making jokes about Ron and about her pregnancy to break the tension. Ike was in the living room, lying on the couch, the satellite remote in one hand. Twenty-one years older than Shelby, he was growing increasingly annoyed by the shrieks of laughter and the giggles coming from the next room. The Wards were driving six hours to Louisville the next morning on a business trip, and Ike wanted the house quiet.

Shelby hadn't told Ike that Susan was going to Pikeville. He would never have agreed to let her go, knowing she was going there for one thing, to see Putnam. Ike wanted Susan to stay away from Putnam and the FBI. The whole affair was bad news as far as he was concerned. So Shelby told Ike that her sister was spending the night with Pam, a neighbor who lived down the street.

When the time came for Susan to leave, she opened her umbrella, and headed for the post office.

She stood out in front for a half-hour before Ron picked her up. He then drove her to the Landmark motel and checked her in, using his own credit card to guarantee that the bill would be paid. Once in her room, Susan did not bother to get herself settled. She called Mark instantly and then went to his room.

The next day, Tommy Estep, a friend of Susan and Kenneth's, called Shelby's, trying to reach Susan. Tommy and his wife knew about her affair with Putnam. They even knew Susan was pregnant by him, and had offered to put her up at their home in Wisconsin—an offer Susan had contemplated accepting in her moments of desperation before Mark's return.

When Susan called her sister from the Landmark on Wednesday, June 7, Shelby relayed Tommy's message, telling her that Estep wanted to meet her and Kenneth in Princeton, West Virginia; that a drug pickup was scheduled. Then she asked about Mark.

"I brought up about child support and everything about the baby," Susan said, "but he just doesn't want to talk about it. He doesn't want to give me anything."

"Well, if you ask me, you're over there making a fool of yourself. He's not going to give you any money, so why don't you come on home now."

But Susan just started laughing.

"Susan, get Ron to bring you home. Get out of there, or let me come and pick you up, and when you come home, don't talk about Mark. You forget about Mark. Block him out of your mind," Shelby pleaded.

Susan called Shelby a number of times from the Landmark during her four-day stay there. She talked about making love with Mark and about what a great body he had. She talked about Ron, and they laughed about Ron's weight. She mentioned that her room was nice, and in one conversation, she said she was folding Mark's clothes and was calling from his room. Susan also told Shelby that Ron had bought her the prettiest shorts set, a blue and white Kentucky Wildcats outfit. "You tell Monica I'll give it to her when I get home," Susan said. "She'll just love it!" Monica is Shelby's daughter.

In her initial conversations with Susan, Shelby says her sister never mentioned threatening Mark. She didn't say anything about going to the FBI or the media in her first days at the Landmark. She did make it clear that Mark was continuing to deny he was the father of her child and was refusing to pay child support or to give her any money for medical checkups. Susan said he was angry because she wouldn't have an abortion.

However, Shelby was becoming worried about Susan's safety. She thought Mark might try to hurt her in some way so she'd lose the baby. But Susan had no fears about that. Apparently she was more worried about Kenneth finding her than about Mark's anger. To Susan, Kenneth was the real threat. She believed he might try to shoot her if he found out she was with Mark in Pikeville.

"Will you check on the kids for me, Shelb?" Susan asked her sister.

"Why, sure. I've just seen them here yesterday. I told you, they're doing just fine. They're with Kenneth."

"You know, Shelby, you've been awfully good to me and I love you, but I dread so much coming back over there, facing Kenneth and Sherri and all

192

of them, I wish there was some place I could take my kids and get away from Kenneth, get away from there. Will you promise me you'll make sure Kenneth's taking care of my kids?"

"Yeah, sure I will, Suzie. But why don't you have Mark bring you home this evening? It's not doing you any good being over there."

"I know. Mark left the room in tears today. He was on his way to meet with Tom Self, that's the federal prosecutor. Me and Mark argued about the baby a lot. We really got into it."

"Well, come on home!"

"No, he said we'd talk about it when he got back, and I believe he's going to get me set up in witness protection."

That same day, Ron Poole took Susan out for a ride over to Letcher County. Poole was serving some papers to witnesses and he took her along just to get her out of her motel room. According to Shelby, it was raining hard that day, and she was surprised that Ron made his way to an outdoor pay phone to call and ask her to come pick up Susan. Ron told Shelby that Mark was furious because Susan was staying at the Landmark. "You need to come over here and get your sister." Ron seemed a bit worried about Susan, Shelby thought, but it never dawned on her that Poole's call might have been an unconscious cry for help.

"My car's in the shop, Ron. The brakes are being worked on, and I can't find a way over to Pikeville today," she told him.

However, after Shelby hung up, she got to thinking and really started to worry about Susan. Shelby had never met Mark Putnam, but she knew how Susan could get to a person. She feared there was no telling what Putnam might do if Susan pushed him too far.

On Thursday, June 8, Susan called Shelby from the Landmark twice, and in Shelby's last conversation with her sister, she implored her to come home, to get away from Putnam.

"I will," Susan said. "I'm going to have Mark bring me back tonight or in the morning."

Friday and Saturday went by, and Shelby heard nothing from Susan. By now she was worried sick. She started to call Mark's room at the Landmark, but decided maybe Susan and Mark needed time alone to work things out.

By Sunday, June 11, Shelby still hadn't heard from Susan, and she was so upset she felt sick and took to her bed. She couldn't shake the feeling that something was drastically wrong, and if anything had happened to her sister she felt it was her fault. She had allowed Susan to go to Pikeville, and she had egged her to push for child support.

She couldn't discuss her fears with her husband because she had lied to him. She could only wait by the phone and pray.

On Sunday evening, Shelby's phone rang at exactly five P.M. She remembers the time because she was staring at the red lights on her digital alarm clock. The call was from Ron Poole.

"Hey, has that sister of yours ever gotten home?" he asked.

"Lord, no! I haven't seen her or heard from her

since Thursday!" Shelby whispered.

"She shoulda been home by now," Poole said.

"You didn't bring her?"

"No. I figured Mark had brought her home and left her at your house!"

"No. I haven't seen Susan at all and I've been worried sick about her. If she came, maybe she's over at Kenneth's."

"Well, you check into it and I'll get back to you. I'm getting a little worried about her now," Poole said casually.

Shelby hung up and called Kenneth, only to discover that Susan hadn't been seen anywhere near Vulcan in days. She tried to determine whether he might have done something to her, but Kenneth denied any knowledge of Susan's whereabouts.

Shelby didn't know that when Ron Poole had checked Susan's room out on Friday, June 9, he had removed her clothing, purse, and makeup from the motel. When Poole called Shelby about Susan on Sunday, he hadn't mentioned that he had found Susan Smith's clothes in her room.

The next morning, Monday, June 12, Poole phoned Shelby again. This time his voice was rough, and he seemed pretty worried about Susan's disappearance.

"Susan's gone and I can't find her," Poole reported. "Her clothes were at the Landmark in a brown paper bag. She left them in her room. I checked with the maid, and she said Susan didn't turn the room key in."

"Her clothes were in a paper bag?" Shelby's voice quivered.

"Yeah. And tennis shoes and makeup. She had a Landmark towel in there, too. The maid found her hairbrush on the sink. Do you have any idea where she could be?"

"Well, Tommy Estep called over here the other day and talked about meeting her at Princeton. Do you think Mark could have brought her up there?"

"I don't know. Maybe that's where she is. I'll ask him."

"You mean Susan left all her clothes there at the Landmark? Was the purple outfit there?"

"Yeah."

"Well, then, what's she wearing? Wait, she told me you bought her a new outfit, a Kentucky Wildcats shorts set. Maybe she's wearing that."

"No, that was in the bag, too."

"Well if all her stuff is there, what in the world is Susan wearing?"

"I don't know. Maybe she had some of Mark's clothes on and just hooked up with the Esteps and got high and ran off."

"But what would she have on her feet? You said her Keds were in the bag too, right?"

"Yeah."

"And you didn't buy her anything else to wear, Ron?"

"No, but maybe she made some money and went out and bought some new clothes and shoes. Who knows?"

"What about her purse? Was that there, too?"

"Yeah. Her purse, her makeup—everything was in her room."

"How about my watch? I gave her my good

watch to wear!"

"That was in the purse."

"Well, it doesn't make sense, her running off and leaving her purse, Ron. She would never do that!"

"Well, I don't know anything more right now, Shelby."

"Well, you better start asking Mark some questions. Maybe Mark knows where she's at."

For the next three days, almost every hour on the hour, Ron Poole called Shelby to check on the whereabouts of Susan Smith, but he got no information that would lead him to her. Oddly enough, Mark Putnam did not call. He had called Susan from Florida. Now he was in Pikeville and had spent days with her at the Landmark, but he didn't try to contact her. That made Shelby suspect that Mark was hiding Susan somewhere, that he might even have sent her to Florida.

On Wednesday, Poole told Shelby that he and Putnam had gone out to eat and he'd questioned Mark about Susan's disappearance. Putnam claimed the last time he saw Susan was Wednesday, June 7, but Shelby knew better because Susan had called her from Mark's motel room on Thursday, June 8. That was the day she'd said Mark had left the room in tears. Shelby knew Mark was lying. She told Ron that. She asked Poole if he had really interrogated Putnam.

"Have you sat down and questioned Mark?" Shelby asked.

"Mark and I talked about it," Ron replied. "And he said Susan told him she was going with Tommy

Estep to see some people in Chicago. He offered to follow her over to Princeton, but Susan said no."

"It doesn't sound right. How would Susan get to Princeton? She didn't have a car over there. Ron, you'd better tell Mark to get on the phone with me and give me some answers. Susan's been missing for a week now."

Whatever Poole said to Putnam must have gotten through, because the next day Shelby's phone rang and Mark Putnam was on the line. He was trying to sound relaxed, but Shelby sensed panic in his voice.

"Is Susan there?" Putnam asked.

"No, Susan's not here, Mark. That's what I want you to tell me. Where she is! Susan's supposed to be with you, and she's not come home. What's going on?"

"Well the only thing I know is Susan said she was going with the Esteps, and I told her to let me or Ron follow her as far as Princeton, but she said no, she wanted to go with them by herself because she thought I might bust them for having all these heavy drugs. I told her to make sure to call me when she got there, but I haven't heard from her yet."

"Well, how did she get to Princeton? Who took her?"

"The Esteps came here and got her, I think."

"How did they know she was in Pikeville? I never told them that, Mark."

"I think Susan called them from here. Didn't you tell her they called you looking for her? That's what she told me the other day."

"Yeah, Tommy Estep called, but he said he didn't want to make the drive down here. He wanted her to meet him in Princeton."

"Well I think she made arrangements with them when I was in Lexington, that's all I know. I don't know when she left, because when I got back, she was already gone. I haven't seen her since Wednesday. She told me if she went she was going to stay up there in Chicago for a while."

"Well, I sure appreciate your calling, Mark."

"Susan is supposed to call me over here in Pikeville, so I'll let you know when I hear from her."

"And would you please have her call me! I'm worried sick!"

"I'll tell her to call you as soon as I hear from her. I hope everything's okay, Shelby. I'm sure she's fine."

For a moment, Shelby felt reassured by Putnam's call, but after a while she got to thinking about the inconsistencies in his replies and she was more frightened than ever. She lit a cigarette and paced back and forth, trying to think things through. It seemed strange that Susan would suddenly run off. Besides, why would she be staying in Chicago? That didn't make any sense. The Esteps lived in Milwaukee. She would be staying with them. Susan didn't know anyone in Chicago anymore.

And how had she gotten to Princeton? Tommy Estep was adamant about not wanting to make the drive to Freeburn, so why would he suddenly be willing to come all the way to Pikeville, an hour more on the road? Susan always met Estep somewhere in West Virginia; Estep never made any trips to Pikeville. And Shelby just didn't believe her sister would run off with the Esteps without saying anything about it. The last thing Susan had said was that Mark was going to drive her home. She hadn't mentioned the Esteps.

The thought that Mark might have done Susan harm crossed Shelby's mind, but she tried to dismiss it. However, when another day passed and she had no word from her sister, she became anxious about Susan's safety. She dreamed that Susan was lying at the bottom of a well, that she was spread out across a bed at the Landmark — naked, dead. By now Shelby was at her wit's end. She couldn't sleep. She couldn't eat. She couldn't get Susan off her mind.

In the days that followed, Shelby continued to pester Ron Poole about finding Susan. She was sure Mark Putnam knew where her sister was, and since Putnam was still in town, she didn't want to let him get away without providing some answers. If he had Susan under witness protection, Shelby wanted to know about it.

When she called the FBI office at about 9:00 A.M. on June 14, she could hear Putnam's voice in the background.

"Ron, how is Mark acting? Suspicious or anything?" Shelby asked.

"No, not that I can see. We haven't gotten any word from Susan yet, have we, Mark?" Poole called out.

"Not yet," Putnam said.

She could tell from Ron Poole's tone that with Putnam there he wasn't going to say too much, so she waited for an hour before she called Poole back. This time Ron was alone in the office.

"Ron, what am I going to do?" she asked. "Should I call the police or what? I mean, I've been letting this thing ride for over a week now!"

"Tell you what, why don't you call Terry Hulse, our supervisor, and tell him that Susan is missing. I'll give you the number in Louisville."

"Do you think he might know where she is?"

"I don't know," Poole said.

"Does he know Mark got Susan pregnant?"

"I don't think so. You talk to him. Wait for a few minutes, so I can phone ahead and tell him to expect your call."

Shelby dialed Hulse in a panic. He took her call immediately and she began screaming at the FBI supervisor, telling Hulse about Mark and Susan's affair, about Susan being pregnant, and blaming Mark for her disappearance. Hulse was furious and got nasty with Shelby on the phone, which only made matters more intense.

"I'm reporting my sister's missing, and that she was last with Mark Putnam. She was an informant. They were having a love affair for two years. She's pregnant . . ."

"Whoa, whoa, whoa, young lady. Slow down. Before you go on, from what I heard, your sister slept around with everything in Pikeville," Hulse told her.

"Listen here buddy, you don't even know my sister. Now I'm telling you she's missing and she's been gone for days, and I think Mark Putnam might have done something to her. I think he might even have killed her."

"Well, if your sister shows up, here's what I'll do. I'll have her tested to see if she's pregnant with Mark Putnam's baby, and if it is his kid, we'll take action. We'll pay for the test — if she shows up, okay? That's all we can do."

"Well what I'm really trying to do is find her," Shelby persisted.

"Well, like I said, if she shows up, in a few weeks we can have a test done, and if the baby is Putnam's, we'll take care of it," and Hulse sat quiet on the phone.

"Well, I'll talk to you later." Shelby hung up, in a state of bewilderment. It was obvious that Hulse did not believe her, and it was evident that he knew something about Susan. He might even have been aware of what was going on between her and Mark.

Shelby called Poole back.

"He didn't want to hear a thing I said. He acted like Susan was some old rat informant, telling lies, and that Mark was Mr. Perfect! So, what do I do now?" Shelby cried.

"Well you probably need to call the Kentucky State Police and report a missing person. That's what I think you should do. Get a pencil, and I'll give you the number," Poole told her.

"Well, where's her clothes you said you found? She was wearing my diamond earrings. Did you find them?"

"No, I didn't see any earrings. I've got to keep her clothes here, Shelby, to turn over to the police."

"Can't I just get my watch back?"

"No. I've got to keep everything."

Agent Poole never told Shelby that on the day he had taken Susan Smith's belongings from the Landmark, he had closed the accounts on the two rooms booked in his name at the motel. Room 224, in Poole's name from June 5 through June 9, and room 230, in Poole's name from May 17 through June 9. Neither was Putnam's room. According to the police record, Putnam stayed in room 126 from June 5 to June 25.

Shelby Ward's call to the Kentucky State Police was logged in at ten-fifty-two A.M. on June sixteenth, and a missing person report was filed. The report was turned over to Detective Richard Ray. A member of the force for over twenty years, Ray had worked with Putnam on the Mac Lockhart case. He returned Shelby's call at twelve noon that day, and grew highly suspicious of Putnam after he heard all that Shelby had to say.

Over the telephone, Detective Ray composed Shelby's statement regarding Susan's trip to Pikeville with Ron Poole on June 5. She was hysterical as she spoke, her voice shrill, and Ray had to continually calm her down to get her entire statement.

First Shelby told him that Susan had a room at the Landmark and that she was five months pregnant by FBI Agent Mark Putnam, who also had a room there. She explained to Ray that Susan wanted Mark to provide child support, that she wanted tests taken to prove the baby was Mark's because he was denying it. Shelby said her sister had been seeing Putnam for about two years and had had a miscarriage in January, 1989, and that baby was also Mark's. Ray also learned that Susan often stayed at Putnam's house while his wife was away, and that she came back to Freeburn wearing Mark's clothing. He found out that Mark had taken Susan for a ride around one of the lakes in the area and had acted like a wild man when they'd discussed Susan's pregnancy. Shelby made it clear that Putnam had scared Susan, and she thought he was capable of harming her sister.

Ray made a note that Putnam should be officially interviewed, while Shelby told him that Agent Ron Poole was in contact with her and was trying to locate Susan. She insisted that Susan would have contacted her or her children if she were all right. She told him that her sister had never run off before, then requested that Agent Putnam be polygraphed.

Detective Ray, a highly decorated police officer, assured Shelby that an all-points bulletin would go out across the United States, and he promised to help find Susan Smith. He asked Shelby to keep him posted if she heard from her sister. But weeks went by and Shelby never heard from Susan or the police. Her only real contact with law enforcement was with Ron Poole, who was chasing false leads in the Freeburn area.

Three days after Shelby's initial call to the police, on June 19, 1989, Susan Smith was officially listed as a missing person. On that day Detective

Richard Ray contacted Tommy Estep in Milwaukee. Estep said he had not seen Susan. He explained that he had spoken to Shelby Ward on the telephone shortly before Susan's disappearance to say he was coming to Princeton, but Susan had not gotten back to him. Estep told Ray that Kenneth Smith had recently called him, so had an FBI Agent. Both men had been trying to locate Susan Smith.

Then on June 20, at twelve-thirty P.M., just days before Mark Putnam was to fly back to Florida, Detectives Kenneth Sloane and Richard Ray interviewed Agent Putnam at the Federal Building in Pikeville.

During the brief interview, Putnam told the detectives he left Pikeville in April, 1989, when he was transferred to Florida. He said Susan Smith was an informant, a witness against Carl "Cat Eyes" Lockhart, and he had known her about two years but had not worked with her since the fall of 1988. He also mentioned that Lockhart's girlfriend, Sherri Justice, had beaten Susan up while her brother watched. Putnam said that Susan was paid nine thousand dollars for being a witness and an informant, and at one time had been given four thousand dollars of that amount to leave the area, but she did not.

Putnam added that Susan's testimony against Cat Eyes and her work on another bank robbery, which involved Pete Blankenship, was causing problems for her at home. Putnam also stated that Kenneth Smith had called him at home to complain about how he and Dan Brennan had used Susan, and Smith had phoned his wife and said that her husband was "fucking" Susan, but Susan had talked to Kathy and denied it. Putnam said he had remained in contact with Susan, that he had called her from Florida "to check on her."

Putnam admitted to police that Susan had told him she was pregnant two weeks before he transferred to Miami, but he claimed she would not tell him who the father was. He said she was "fucking Ron Poole or Gary Davis"—Davis, a US Probation Officer, was once a close friend of Putnam—and revealed that he and Susan had discussed her having an abortion when she arrived at the Landmark on June 5. Putnam offered to help her get money for one, but Susan did not want to have an abortion. He claimed that he asked to feel her stomach, but Susan jumped away. According to Putnam, Agent Poole had brought Susan to Pikeville on that date to do some undercover work for him, and Susan was "having problems at home over it." He said that Kenneth was blaming Agent Dan Brennan and him for Susan's problems at home.

He then told the detectives that Susan Smith had called his room at two-thirty A.M. on June 7, waking him out of a deep sleep after he had returned from a trip to Lexington. She had been in contact by phone with some drug dealers from Chicago, and was going to meet them in Princeton, West Virginia. He offered to follow her there in case there was any trouble, but Susan wanted to go alone. He then said that he went back to Lexington on Thursday, June 8, and when he returned, at about two A.M., his informant, "Charlie," who was staying at the motel, told him "the girl"—Susan—had left. Putnam stated that he had not heard from Susan since, though Agent Poole was trying to locate her. He added that Poole was going to let Susan stay at the motel as long as she felt necessary.

He denied that Susan had ever said she was pregnant by him and expressed a willingness to cooperate in the missing person case in any way he could. He was not at the motel on Friday, he said, because he attended a hearing during the day and went to a movie—*Roadhouse*—that night. Putnam added that, on Saturday morning, Ron Poole asked if he had seen Susan, but he hadn't known where she was, only that she'd mentioned some guys from Chicago—"the amigos"—and a Spanish cop she'd been dealing drugs with. Putnam was calm as he spoke with the police, and he walked out of the post with head held high.

On June 23, Richard Ray questioned Agent Ron Poole, who was now telling a different story, claiming that Susan had gone to the Landmark for the sole purpose of discussing her pregnancy and never mentioning any "undercover" work. He told Ray that he drove Susan over to the motel "so she and Mark could work this out," that he rented the room for her "so she would not have to pay for it." Poole said Susan left on Thursday, June 8, "sometime in the evening," and he claimed he didn't know where she was or who had driven her from the motel. He had talked with Putnam at one P.M. on June 13, and Putnam had said he would come back for a polygraph whenever they needed him to. Nothing in Poole's statement could be used as actual evidence by Ray to call Putnam back in. For the moment, his hands were tied.

Then on July 6, Kentucky State Police contacted Deputy Sheriff Burt Hatfield, who said he'd known Susan Smith and that she'd been helping the FBI on bank-robbery cases. Hatfield also knew that Susan had been pregnant and had said the baby was Mark's.

Police then checked Susan's medical and dental records, and discovered that after her miscarriage in January 1989, she'd had a D&C performed by Dr. Song Kim in South Williamson, Kentucky. The records also revealed that she had been given a pregnancy test at the Pike County Health Department, and at the time of her disappearance, she was almost five months pregnant. According to Dr. Mary Fox of the Health Department Susan's delivery date was November 19, 1989.

On July 12, Shelby called the Kentucky State Police in Pikeville and again requested that Agent Mark Putnam be polygraphed. Unfortunately, her request met with evasive answers. "We're going to have to sit on the fence for a while," one officer told her. "We need evidence. All we have right now is a bunch of false leads." By this time Shelby was frustrated and sure that law enforcement had abandoned their pursuit of Mark Putnam.

Then, out of nowhere, the Kentucky State Police focused the investigation on Shelby. Now she was being asked to come in and take a polygraph to clear herself. The police insinuated that she and Susan might have some kind of game going on, that they might be hiding Susan in order to get Putnam in trouble. That came as a shock to Shelby, but she consented to taking the lie detector test because she was at that point where she would have done just about anything to accelerate the investigation.

On August 22, when Shelby Ward went down to the Kentucky State Police Post to take her polygraph examination, she sat in a room facing a mirrored wall. She was increasingly nervous as the polygraph proceeded, listening to the needle move across the paper on the machine which sat directly behind her. Shelby did not recall the entire exam, which was never attached to police files, but she was certain that Mark Putnam's name never came up.

When the exam was over, Charles Hines, the examiner, found that Shelby was being truthful and did not know where her sister was.

"I want Mark Putnam polygraphed. You said you would polygraph him within a week," Shelby blurted out to the police when she heard she had passed the lie detector test.

"We'll get to it, but we have to get Kenneth Smith out of the way," one of the detectives responded.

Shelby insisted that Kenneth Smith had not done anything to her sister, that he hadn't known Susan was staying at the Landmark.

But the police thought differently.

According to their investigative strategy, Kenneth Smith was a prime suspect in the case because he was being viewed as a jealous ex-husband. Shelby learned from the police of Putnam's assertion that Smith was angry about Susan's informant work, which accounted for their belief that Smith was a suspect in Susan's disappearance. In addition, Kenneth Smith seemed to be hiding from the law. He could not be found, and this was holding up the police investigation.

If Kenneth Smith was hiding, no one was searching very hard for him, Shelby told them, because he and his children were still in and around the Freeburn area, living with Tennis Daniels at one point and with his brother Roy at another. Ironically, for most of the five-month period the police were allegedly "searching" for Smith, his family claims he was serving a home-incarceration sentence for drunk driving. Housebound, and living next door to Billy Joe Daniels, he was wearing an electronic bracelet. If he moved more than a hundred and fifty feet from the corresponding device in the telephone, a buzzer would sound at a monitoring station and marshals would be called.

This gives some credence to Shelby's complaint that the police didn't treat Susan's case seriously. Other cases took precedence in their unit, and months passed before they focused on Susan's disappearance.

"She just wasn't important enough for them to bother to do anything about it, and here was Mark Putnam, this big FBI agent, and they were afraid to question him," Shelby later explained.

At the time, she had no way of knowing that Kentucky State Police had to follow a certain procedure before they could approach Putnam. They had to make all the right moves and keep gathering facts, eliminating all other possible suspects before they could seriously consider Putnam as the prime suspect. After all, the Kentucky State Police had very little evidence. There was no body. There were no witnesses. They had to be reasonably sure of their suspicions before making such a serious allegation against a federal agent.

Shelby, still in contact with Ron Poole every day, reminded him that in one of her last phone conversations with her sister, Susan had mentioned leaving the Landmark with Mark to go to Virginia to serve some papers. Shelby thought Susan might be in Virginia; Mark might have hidden her in that state. But Ron told her he'd questioned Mark about the Virginia excursion, and Putnam had denied that Susan had gone anywhere with him.

Putnam, now back at work in Florida, repeatedly told Kentucky State Police that he would fly up to take a polygraph "anytime." Meanwhile, Ron Poole was unable to find Susan, unable to get anything useful out of Mark, and unable to clear himself of any connection with Susan's disappearance.

At one point Poole told Shelby, "I'll tell you, it's starting to make me look bad, this whole thing, and every time I talk to Mark about a polygraph, he changes the subject. I told him I was willing to take a polygraph myself and asked him to come up and take the thing so we could get on with the investigation, but Mark just didn't want to talk about it . . ."

Chapter Twelve

By late August, Shelby realized that nothing was being done to find her sister. In her anger and disgust, she got Kentucky State Police Captain Gary Rose on the phone and threatened to go to the press unless Putnam took a polygraph. Rose told her they needed more time to do a thorough investigation; he asked her to be patient.

But Shelby was insistent. "Well, why can't we put Susan's picture on the TV? They do that all the time when someone's missing!"

Captain Rose remained firm. He said that state police were in constant contact with the FBI and that any press coverage would jeopardize their efforts.

Shelby wasn't buying it. She had discovered that the Pike County prosecutor's office remained uninformed about the Susan Smith case, and she believed Rose was skirting the issue. The KSP was foot-dragging, she complained, and insisted that it was time the newspapers printed Susan's picture. This, at least, could be done, she urged.

Rose told Shelby that he needed to polygraph Kenneth Smith before he could get to Mark Putnam. After all, he said, Shelby had supplied police with pictures of Susan covered in mud and information on the warrant Susan had obtained for Kenneth's arrest in May, 1989. According to Rose, Kenneth Smith was considered a prime suspect, and he still hadn't been administered a polygraph. Kenneth Smith had to come to Pikeville for a lie detector test, he reminded her.

In the ensuing months, it seemed that nothing much was being done to accelerate the progress of the Susan Smith case. Periodically, Shelby received a phone call from the dispatcher at the Pikeville post. Sometimes the officer on the line would ask her if she knew where Kenneth was, if she had seen him. Shelby couldn't understand why the police hadn't been able to find Kenneth Smith. To her, they seemed to be stalling.

As the months went by, Shelby waited for someone to call her and provide some answers. She was unable to concentrate on anything else. In her increasing despair, she closed her beauty shop and started downing antidepressants. She conjured up images of Susan, trying desperately to believe that her sister was alive. And she was in constant contact with Ron Poole. At one point, Poole called her and said he had been to a fortuneteller. He claimed this woman told him Susan was "somewhere far, far away." Shelby got her hopes up after Poole's call. She thought Susan might just be in hiding and might appear at any moment.

In all her confusion, Shelby thought she was going crazy, and she began going to a psychologist, saying that she was obsessed with discovering Susan's whereabouts, explaining that her sister was always in her dreams—Susan was crawling up a hill, Susan was reaching out to her and then sliding back into darkness before Shelby could grab her. Indeed, Shelby's life had become one long nightmare, and there was no resolution in sight.

Meanwhile, Susan's brother, Billy Joe searched for Susan week in and week out, questioning people, showing strangers Susan's picture, checking to see if she'd been in Virginia or West Virginia. He even followed cars across state lines whenever he spotted someone inside who looked like Susan. Soon a number of Freeburn people came up with stories about having seen his missing sister, which only made matters worse. Too many people from the area wanted to play a role in the missing person drama. Too many claimed to have the resolution, but they did not.

By mid November, 1989, the time when Susan was due to give birth to Putnam's child, Shelby was almost certain that her sister was dead. Meanwhile police were doing almost nothing about it, and she was outraged. Every few weeks, the police would call her to say they were updating their files and to ask if Shelby had heard from her sister. "No I haven't," Shelby would say in a huff. "You're supposed to be trying to find her."

Then, just as the Thanksgiving holiday approached, something strange occurred which altered the case and almost halted the investigation: a report came in that Susan Smith had made a number of calls to Josie Thorpe, one of her female friends in Freeburn.

When Thorpe told people that Susan was calling to ask about Kenneth and the kids, the news had traveled like wildfire throughout the Tug Valley. As soon as Shelby heard it, she went over and questioned Thorpe herself.

"Susan's been calling you, I hear! Is that right, Josie?"

"She says it's Susan," Thorpe told her.

"Did you ask Susan why she hasn't been calling me?" Shelby wanted to know.

"She told me she wore your necklace and your earrings, and she was afraid you might be mad at her, so she was going to wait a while before she called you," Thorpe said.

"Well, what all did she talk about? Do you know where she is?"

"No, when I asked her where she was, she hung up."

"What did she call you for?" Shelby persisted.

"She told me she had left some clothes in a garbage bag at your house, some pants that have elastic in them, big enough so I can wear them. And she said she had some orange nail polish that she didn't want. She told me to come down to your place and tell you to let me have that bag. She said I could have them."

When Thorpe mentioned the orange nail polish, Shelby was suddenly convinced that Susan was, indeed, alive. As far as she was concerned, nobody else knew about that ghastly orange nail polish. It had to be Susan calling.

Shelby's heart raced as she rushed home to call Ron Poole, all the while remembering the laughs she and Susan had had over that nail polish. Shelby had made fun of Susan for wearing it when she'd gone to see Mark, and soon after, Susan had tossed the stuff into a bag of old clothes she intended to discard, telling Shelby she was right, the color didn't suit her.

And as soon as Ron Poole got the information about the call to Thorpe, he went up to Josie's place and questioned her about the nail polish and the clothing, but he learned nothing of significance regarding Susan's whereabouts. After a brief conversation, Poole gave Thorpe his card, telling her to contact him if the woman called back.

Then another call came in from "Susan Smith." This time Thorpe assured the woman caller that Kenneth and the kids were fine, explaining to "Susan" that she had just been over to see them the day before. "Susan" made mention of a swan figurine that she had given Thorpe as a gift, asking whether Thorpe was still keeping flowers in the porcelain figure. Thorpe again asked where "Susan" was calling from, and the woman on the phone said she wasn't allowed to say. She made Thorpe promise not to tell the police or anybody else about her calls.

But Thorpe called Shelby, who relayed the information to Poole. He decided they should put a tape recorder on Thorpe's phone, and he brought one to Freeburn the next day. Shelby promptly went over to Thorpe's and hooked up the apparatus, explaining over and over again how to work the device. After it was installed, Thorpe never received another call from "Susan."

When Shelby questioned Ron Poole about whether Mark Putnam knew about the wire tap, Ron said, "Yeah, I told him about the calls that came in, and I told him we put a recorder on the phone. Mark just said uh-huh and went on to the next subject."

"Oh, you stupid thing!" Shelby scolded. "Don't you know that it could have been Mark behind making those calls!"

But Poole avoided the issue, telling Shelby to report the calls to the Kentucky State Police. Shelby immediately phoned Gary Rose. When the police contacted Thorpe, she agreed to make a statement to Detective Ray over the phone. In this conversation, it came out that Thorpe's telephone number was unlisted and she had only had it for about six months. Thorpe contended that she had never talked to Susan by phone before, but that the voice had sounded like Susan's. She said she'd received three or four calls, each about a month apart, from a woman who had claimed to be Susan Smith. Thorpe said "Susan Smith" never stayed on the phone long, talking for only a couple of minutes, and she added that the woman never mentioned the kids or any other relative by name.

Thorpe also told police that "Susan Smith" said that she left some fingernail polish and a sweater at her sister's, and told Thorpe she could have them, explaining that the woman "would not stay on the line long enough for me to tell her to call Shelby."

The "Susan Smith" calls probably resulted in the

investigation being placed on hold, Rose later claimed, because, in November, Shelby Ward had called him and was "totally convinced" that Susan was alive.

"Shelby based the strength of her comment on the fact that Josie Thorpe had mentioned a specific nail polish and clothes that no one else could have known about," Rose said. "Shelby even commented on canceling the investigation." However, Shelby vehemently denies Rose's contention. "I did think Susan was alive," she admitted, "but I never wanted the investigation stopped. I wanted Susan found."

In any event, because of the "Susan Smith" calls, the investigation was put on hold until Christmas. Kentucky State Police believed it probably was Susan calling, and their hypothesis was reinforced when yet another call came in from "Susan Smith" just before Christmas. This call was made to Helen Prater, an acquaintance of Susan's in the Freeburn area.

As soon as Susan's family learned of the call, Ron Poole and Billy Joe Daniels went to the Prater place to question Helen about the voice on the telephone. Prater told Poole that the caller had sounded like Susan and had asked for her son by name, but she admitted she wasn't sure the caller was Susan, and she reported that when she asked where Susan was calling from, the woman hung up. Poole and Bo Daniels left Prater's place in a state of bewilderment. Bo began to believe that Susan was alive, but when he asked Poole what he thought, Poole would give him no direct answer.

By mid December 1989, between the phone calls and the rumors going around Freeburn that Susan Smith had been spotted in Matewan, in Phelps, and in other nearby towns, everyone in Susan's family believed she was still alive, hiding out with Mark Putnam and her newborn baby.

But when Christmas came and went without a call or card from Susan, her family members became distressed. Susan was not the type of person to forget them, especially her kids, at Christmas. Still, if she was under witness protection, maybe she hadn't been allowed to make contact, they thought. No one in the family knew what the witness protection rules were.

As for the Kentucky State Police, they weren't even sure a crime had been committed. For all they knew Susan Smith could have run away, plain and simple. Shelby Ward and Mark Putnam had both relayed information about her planned meeting with out-of-state drug dealers.

The police had only allegations that Susan had been sleeping with Putnam, no proof. The fact that Ron Poole suspected the affair had been going on was certainly not enough to proceed on. And even if Putnam had been having an affair with Smith, that would not make him a murder suspect.

To complicate their problems with the case, the police were unable to ascertain the FBI's position in the matter. Though the FBI was in constant contact with Ron Poole, the police weren't told whether Poole was doing an official or unofficial investigation. Poole was being evasive about the whole business, and the police were getting almost no cooperation from the FBI.

"Ron was doing a lot of things here, trying to locate Susan, but nobody at the FBI came out and told us that he was working in an official capacity. Ron was making a lot of phone calls, we knew that," Captain Rose said. "We later learned that he wasn't doing an official investigation for the FBI."

On January 25, 1990, Sergeant Don Gill contacted Inez Hall at the Landmark Inn and obtained a copy of the bill for the room Susan Smith had occupied during June, 1989. Only three long-distance calls had been made from the room, all to Shelby Ward. He also discovered that Ron Poole had paid for the room, and at that point Gill called Shelby, telling her, "This case is now top priority. I'm on to something, and everybody's a suspect as far as I'm concerned!"

Gill insinuated that there had been a "coverup," and he promised to check into everyone's role in the affair, swearing that he would "get to the bottom of it."

Not long after Gill's call, however, Shelby discovered that he had been transferred out of the Pikeville post, and the investigation continued without him.

KSP detectives interviewed the Landmark chambermaid, Georgia Ann Little, who said that Susan had stayed in her room most of the time and that after Susan had left, she'd found a purse and a plastic bag with clothing and some makeup in it. Inez Hall, the front desk clerk, told police that Ron Poole had taken Smith's items with him when he'd left the motel on June 9, 1989.

In late January 1990, Kenneth Smith was located and voluntarily went to the Pikeville post to take a polygraph and make a statement about his ex-wife. In his statement to Detective Ray, Kenneth said he'd been married to Susan for three and a half years and had lived with her after their divorce until March of 1989. He stated that she had been working with Agent Mark Putnam on the bank-robbery case involving Cat Eyes Lockhart and that she'd driven to Pikeville real often, supposedly because she was working with Mark or buying drugs.

Kenneth also revealed that Susan had said she and Mark loved each other and that he had called Putnam's wife on three separate occasions and had told her about the affair. Just a few nights before Susan had disappeared, Kenneth claimed she had come to Vulcan and they had decided to get back together. But he denied seeing her since. According to Kenneth, Susan had told him she was pregnant about three weeks before she left, saying she had discussed the pregnancy with Mark and he had agreed to pay child support.

Kenneth assured police that he did not know where Susan was, but Josie Thorpe had heard from her and had come to his house because Susan had wanted her to give the children a kiss and a hug. He said he did not do anything to Susan, that he believed she was alive and in Florida with Mark Putnam.

After Kenneth made his statement to police, he took a polygraph in Pikeville — and failed it.

Police deemed the test invalid, however, after Kenneth admitted that he had taken valium before the examination. They asked him to take the test again, and on January 29, Kenneth agreed to be administered a second polygraph, but this time in Frankfort, Kentucky, where Lieutenant Phil Woods, one of the state's top polygraphists, would run two tests on him.

When both procedures had been completed, Woods told Detective Kenneth Sloane that even though Smith had taken some valium earlier, he considered him a "good reactor," and in his opinion, Smith had not told the complete truth during the test. So now Kenneth found himself under fire and had no way to prove his innocence.

Smith vividly recalls that Woods was convinced he had killed Susan. In fact, during questioning, Woods pulled up a chair, sitting on it backwards, and stared into Kenneth's eyes, then telling him how and why he had killed his ex-wife:

"You lied about every fucking thing," Woods accused. "Why don't you just go ahead and admit it, get it out of your system. Everybody's got a breaking point. You just found out about her sleeping with Putnam and you couldn't stand it and you killed her."

"I told the damn truth," Kenneth snapped.

"Everybody's got a breaking point. You've got one. Nobody could put up with that — I'd probably lose it. What's your breaking point?"

"Evidently I didn't reach it."

"Why don't you get it off your chest? I know you want to tell somebody. One thing led to another.

You slapped her first, then you jumped on her—can you remember? Did you drown her?"

"I'm telling you, I didn't do anything to her!"

"Come on, what's your breaking point?" Woods kept repeating.

"I did not do anything to Susan! I'm telling you the truth! Now what else do you want me to say?" Kenneth quipped.

By the time he left Frankfort, it was obvious to Kenneth that the law was trying to pin Susan's disappearance on him. He was infuriated because he felt the police should be investigating Putnam, not him.

Nonetheless, on February 21, Kenneth subjected himself to a third polygraph exam, this time in Pikeville. To prevent him from taking any kind of drug which might affect the results, the night before the test he was put up at a local motel under the guard of a state trooper.

Even though the test results of the third examination were ruled inconclusive, Hines told Captain Rose that he believed Smith was telling the truth, that he had nothing to do with the disappearance of Susan Smith. The focus of the investigation then shifted from Kenneth Smith.

Now Special Agent Mark Putnam became the number-one suspect.

Through the end of January, 1990, Putnam had assured his supervisor, Terry Hulse, that he would take a polygraph exam "whenever necessary." He was kept abreast of the investigation being conducted in Pikeville, but remained very cool about the Susan Smith case, acting as though he was only vaguely interested. Usually he was too involved on drug stings and other FBI operations in Miami to talk at length to anyone about Smith's disappearance.

However, when Kentucky State Police, in early February, officially requested that Putnam take a polygraph, he evaded their calls and suddenly refused to cooperate. That was the official response that came back to Captain Gary Rose via Terry Hulse on February 2, 1990.

At that point Richard Ray's suspicions about Putnam were confirmed. From the time the investigation had begun, Ray believed Putnam's transfer was linked with Susan's pregnancy and with her disappearance. Ray also wondered why Ron Poole seemed so concerned about what had happened and why he had remained in constant contact with Shelby Ward. Did Poole know what Putnam had done with Smith? Ray didn't have the answers, but he knew things didn't look good for Putnam.

Now that Mark Putnam had refused to come to Kentucky for an interview, Captain Rose called Major Jerry Lovitt, the branch commander of the state police posts in eastern Kentucky, to ask for travel vouchers. Rose and Lovitt were good friends and the branch commander had been kept apprised about the Susan Smith case in an unofficial capacity up until that point, all the while thinking that Putnam had to have been an innocent victim of rumor and gossip.

"For a long time all I did was function as a

sounding board for Captain Rose. I was caught completely off guard when I first heard about it, like everyone else," Lovitt said. "I mean, here's our number one law enforcement agency, the one that's held up as an example for the rest of us. And you have a tendency to think, well, here's a young girl described as unstable. She has probably run away somewhere."

But in early Feburary when Rose informed him of Putnam's sudden reluctance to cooperate and of his own suspicions about the young agent, Lovitt became convinced that Putnam had done something to Susan Smith. Without a body, however, there was no clear homicide, and Putnam couldn't be indicted.

"Until we can produce the body, we have nothing," Lovitt told Rose.

As part of the missing person investigation the police contacted Donna Charles, Susan's friend. During her interview, Charles told police that she had been with Susan Smith seven or eight times when Susan had met with Mark Putnam. Charles said she and Susan had been in the FBI office with Ron Poole, Mark Putnam, and Don Lafferty, the US Marshal; and she alluded to her knowledge of Mark and Susan's affair. But she divulged no further information.

On February 5, Charles Trotter, a witness in the auto theft trial, was called in to meet with Captain Gary Rose and Lieutenant Paul Maynard at the Pikeville Post. Trotter, who was put up at the Landmark Inn while Susan Smith was there in June, 1989, told police he'd stayed at the motel for five months, remaining for two months after Susan disappeared.

He remembered the day Ron Poole had brought Susan to the motel and checked her in, remembered talking to Mark about her and Mark's telling him Susan was going to check out. He didn't get the impression that Mark was "fooling around" with Susan, but he did feel that she was "coming on" to Mark; Mark had told Trotter that Susan called his room a lot.

Trotter said that, on the morning Putnam was leaving to go talk to Tom Self, Mark told him Susan had gone to his room and may have made some phone calls from there. Trotter said he never saw anyone talk to Susan except Mark Putnam and Ron Poole. He did not recall telling Mark the girl was gone or that her purse had been left in the room.

Trotter told police he saw Ron and Susan come out of the bank across from the FBI office at nine A.M. on June 8. Around noon that same day, Trotter was looking out his motel window and saw Ron pull up to the motel office with Susan. She stayed in the Bronco and Poole came out with a receipt in his hand and then pulled on into the motel. Not long after Poole came out alone and left in his Bronco.

Trotter told police he saw Susan Smith at the Landmark that same evening. He did not know she was pregnant. He said the maid collected some items from Susan's room after it was vacated.

Trotter did not assert to police that he was aware of any foul play on the part of the FBI, but Georgia

Ann Little, the chambermaid, would later recount Trotter's words to her when Susan came up missing: "They've got her!" he had gasped.

On March 6, a teletype arrived on the National Crime Information Service. An unidentified female had been found along Interstate 75 in Tennessee. The remains bore some similarities to Susan Smith, so Dr. Richard Greene of Pikeville was called upon to make a chart of Susan Smith's dental records. Shelby was then contacted by Richard Ray to see whether a positive ID could be made.

"The woman who was found had fake nails," Ray said. "Did Susan wear fake fingernails?"

"No," Shelby told the detective. "Susan has beautiful nails. She's never needed to wear fake ones."

The young woman on I-75 was just another dead end.

By mid March of 1990 Kentucky State Police were finally ready to move in on Putnam, but they now found that the FBI was not cooperating in allowing them to investigate Putnam on their own. John Paul Runyon, the Pike County Commonwealth Attorney, was contacted and given a full report of the Susan Smith case history. Runyon, who has handled over two hundred murder cases in his career as an attorney, could give them advice that would prove invaluable, police thought.

However John Paul Runyon reminded Pike County detectives that even if Putnam submitted to a polygraph, and the polygraph showed he was guilty, in the state of Kentucky, polygraphs were not admissible as evidence in court. They were an investigative tool only. With no body and only circumstantial evidence, there wasn't much of a case against Putnam.

And it wasn't until late March, nine months after Susan's disappearance, that Runyon called Shelby Ward to arrange a meeting at his Pikeville office. She was asked to be there early in the morning to meet with Runyon and members of the Kentucky State Police. No one in the FBI would be at the meeting, she was told, because the FBI was not yet officially involved in the case. Present at the meeting were Shelby Ward, Gary Rose, Richard Ray, and Paul Maynard, all of the KSP. They talked in Runyon's massive library for over an hour.

Runyon, a tall, imposing white-haired man, had served as Commonwealth Attorney for twenty-eight years. He was a man with a lot of clout in eastern Kentucky. If anyone could get the job done, KSP believed, Runyon could. He is a man filled with bravado, one who takes every opportunity to let people know that he goes hunting with the governor of Kentucky, who likes to remind people that in World War II, he had his ear pierced when he crossed the China Sea, in accordance with Navy tradition.

During their initial meeting, Shelby told Runyon about Susan's affair with Putnam and the pregnancy. His immediate response was to lean back in his chair, look at Captain Rose, and say, "Has anybody ever thought about tailing Mark down in Florida—to see where he goes and what he does?"

"No, we never thought about that," Rose admitted.

"Well, why don't we do that? Why don't we send somebody down to follow him around and see what he's up to."

By the time Shelby's meeting with Runyon ended, the Commonwealth Attorney promised that he would take care of the matter, asking Shelby to contact him if she heard anything from Susan.

"What about Mark Putnam taking a lie-detector test?" Shelby asked before she left.

"We'll get on it," Runyon said.

"Before I walked out, John Paul was talking about calling Geraldo Rivera if the FBI didn't get the ball rolling," Shelby recalls.

While she had been upstairs in the library with Runyon and the police, her brother, Billy Joe, waiting for her down in the lobby, had overheard the call that came in from Ron Poole. The receptionist had said, "Sorry, Agent Poole, the Commonwealth Attorney is in a meeting right now."

When Shelby joined Billy Joe he immediately told her about the call, and the idea that she was being checked up on started to spook her. "I felt like Poole was following my every move," she declared. "Like I was constantly being watched."

In April, as a last resort, Shelby called her sister, Carla Dean, in Porter, Texas. Carla said she hadn't seen Susan, but Shelby insisted to police that it was possible Susan was hiding out with her, that Carla might be "covering" for Susan. A picture of Susan

Smith was sent to the Montgomery County Texas Sheriff's Office on April 16, 1990, but a reply from Texas showed that officers checked the given address, only to find that the Deans had moved and could not be located.

In the meantime, John Paul Runyon was getting conflicting reports. Shelby had been adamant about Susan's exclusive affair with Putnam, yet the local police alleged that Susan had had flings with other men in Pikeville. Runyon knew Susan was not the upstanding young woman Shelby was making her out to be, and he suspected Susan might have been killed because she was using the pregnancy to dig her hooks into Putnam.

Moreover, Runyon thought the FBI had no business ignoring the case. He didn't like the idea that the Bureau was putting up a wall, and it didn't wear well with him that the FBI would use an informant as long as they had, would let her testify in court against a dangerous criminal, and then would ignore her disappearance. Runyon contemplated the ramifications of an FBI agent's affair with an informant becoming public knowledge. He pictured cases being overturned, falling like dominoes, because of the Putnam/Smith affair. In any event, it was now over nine months since Susan Smith's disappearance, and Runyon knew this was no longer just a missing-person case. It was a serious problem that the FBI could not just sweep under the carpet.

"I mean, the FBI flat ignored the case," Runyon later told a magazine reporter. "Ron Poole sort of put on a superficial charade like he was investigating, but God damn it, he wasn't. He didn't talk to me or anybody else."

Runyon told the interviewer "the FBI kept misdirecting police," saying that he finally sat down with the chief agent from Louisville, Terry O'Conner, and the two of them argued about everything. Runyon claimed O'Conner tried to remain aloof and disinterested and recounted his words to Agent O'Conner.

"I said, look, this is your case. You people are involved in it up to your eyeballs. If one of my assistants had an informant, and all of a sudden she disappeared, you'd think a bomb had been dropped on this office. I'd get everybody on lie detectors. I'd turn this place upside down. You people threw this girl to the wolves. And if you don't start moving on this case soon, you're likely to see someone like Geraldo Rivera coming through your door."

Within days of Runyon's conversation with O'Conner, Special Agent Terry Hulse was sent the KSP report on Susan Daniels Smith, which he eventually forwarded to FBI headquarters in Washington.

About six weeks later, two people flew to Pikeville from Washington, one an FBI agent, the other from the justice department. Kentucky State Police and John Paul Runyon went over every detail of the case with them. They flew back to Washington and returned to Pikeville on the first of May, to begin a joint FBI–KSP investigation on the case.

On May 7, Senior Special Agent Jim Huggins

was put in charge of the internal FBI investigation. He became the agent responsible for keeping tabs on all interviews and reports from the nine FBI agents he had assigned to the case. At first, the FBI was looking at it as a possible kidnapping, because they didn't know what had happened to Susan Smith. If it was a murder case, that would be a state violation, not a federal matter.

"We got involved because Putnam was an employee," Huggins explained. "We looked at it as a kidnapping because that's the only way we could investigate it. In other words, if we found a body in West Virginia, or some other state, then it would be kidnapping, so that's the jurisdiction we used to get into this thing."

On the first day of his assignment, Huggins went to the Landmark Inn, accompanied by Special Agents Tim Adams and Bill Welsh of the FBI. The chambermaid, Georgia Ann Little, was reinterviewed. Her story was essentially the same one she had told Richard Ray.

Huggins then received permission from the motel owner to go through the records. He and his team reported to state police that there were receipts in both Poole's and Putnam's names for May 23 and 24. His team also reported that Putnam had room 126 from June 5 through June 25, and that Poole had room 224 from June 5 through June 9. There was no mention in the Kentucky State Police report that Huggins had found any record of the room Poole had rented from May 17 through June 9, room 230, for which Poole paid over twelve hundred dollars in cash two days before Putnam left town.

On May 10, Huggins contacted the Hertz rental company and learned that Putnam had rented a Ford Tempo on June 5, 1989. He'd returned this car on June 11 because the windshield was cracked and had obtained another Tempo, which he kept until June 25.

Mary June Baker, a Hertz employee, was then contacted about the damage to the first rental car Putnam had used. She said Putnam had told her that coal had fallen from a truck on US Highway 23 and had cracked the windshield. FBI Agent Welsh went to Charleston, West Virginia, to obtain the complete records, and the original Ford Tempo was soon located and sent to the FBI lab in Washington for inspection.

Soon thereafter, Huggins' team confirmed, by obtaining copies of Susan Smith's phone bills, that numerous calls had been made between Freeburn and Florida. They also noted the large number of calls made from Freeburn to Pikeville. The FBI team then went to the Pike County Health Department and obtained a copy of Susan Smith's positive pregnancy test slip.

Now that the FBI was involved, a number of people were interviewed again, and copies of records were obtained a second time. Much had to be redone. As the investigation intensified, as many as eighteen people were working on the case, ten from the FBI and eight from the Kentucky State Police.

Burt Hatfield and Ike Ward were both interviewed by the FBI team, as were Josie Thorpe and

Bo Daniels, but all had solid stories. The FBI could find no inconsistencies. By now everything seemed to point to one person — Special Agent Mark Steven Putnam.

On May 8, Richard Ray appeared at Shelby Ward's door with Special Agents Sam Smith and Tom Gayheart. The men sat down at her kitchen table and interviewed her for about four hours, going over every last detail about the calls made to her and about Putnam's contentions and Susan's last words.

At the end of the interview, Agent Sam Smith turned to her and said, "Shelby, I'm going to ask you something, but you don't have to answer me if you don't want to. Where do you think your sister is, and what do you think happened to her?"

"I think my sister is in Florida, or I think Mark killed her," Shelby said flatly.

Shelby handed Ray a pair of men's green, swim trunk-type shorts and told him that Susan had worn them home once from a meeting with Mark. She said her sister had also worn one of Mark's cut-off shirts, but she'd looked around the house and couldn't find it.

When Kenneth Smith was finally located and reinterviewed by the FBI, he reiterated his story and was then served a fugitive warrant for a theft in West Virginia and was taken to the Mingo County West Virginia jail.

Detective Ray, meanwhile, contacted Kelsey Friend, Jr., and discovered that Kenneth Smith had brought in tapes, claiming that they would prove his wife and an FBI agent were having an affair. Friend said neither he nor his secretary had listened to the tapes, that he'd kept them for a while and then had returned them to Kenneth Smith. The tapes now were missing.

About a week after their visit to Shelby, FBI agents went up to Barrenshea Creek and talked to Susan's parents, Sid and Tracy Daniels. It was May 16, nearly a year after the disappearance of their daughter, and the first time that the Daniels had ever been contacted regarding her whereabouts. They felt utterly violated and hinted that Susan had been treated pretty much like a lost dog. The Daniels distrusted the FBI, the police, and the whole investigation, believing that Susan's case had been deliberately overlooked by law enforcement officials.

In timid, shaking voices, they told the agents they had not heard from Susan since May, 1989. The FBI team asked if the Daniels had a hairbrush of Susan's, but neither of her parents could locate one.

"Why don't you all look at the hairbrush Susan left at the Landmark?" Sid asked. He had been told that one of Susan's hairbrushes was being held as evidence. The FBI wanted a second one. Sid didn't understand their line of thinking. He didn't see why one hairbrush wouldn't be enough, nor did he comprehend why it had taken them this long to bother to look for his daughter. Ultimately, Sid had no answers for the FBI men, just accusations and questions, and the only thing the agents left the Daniels' house with was the address of Susan's sister, Carla Dean, now living in Humble, Texas.

This would prove to be another dead-end lead.

Throughout the investigation, Huggins wasn't convinced of Mark Putnam's involvement in any wrongdoing, and the senior FBI man never thought the day would come when he'd be accusing a fellow agent of a crime.

"In this case, I made the decision to go see Mark. I figured we'd resolve that issue, we'd wash him out, and then we'd go to the real guy," Huggins said. "I thought there certainly were a lot of circumstances that pointed toward Mark — that we had to resolve, but I thought, gosh, I can't believe an agent would ever do something like this."

Chapter Thirteen

Meanwhile, back in Sunrise, Florida, all had not been going too well for Special Agent Mark Putnam. Kathy Putnam later told a reporter that he had had diarrhea for a year. She said in the middle of the night Mark would dig and scratch at his chest, and when she shook him, he'd awake, in terror, asking, "What did I say?"

While on assignment for the FBI, Putnam would find himself driving at a hundred miles per hour, his mind a blur. His mental anguish was interfering with his work, and reportedly, in the middle of interviewing a suspect, Putnam got so overwrought he was unable to complete his line of questioning. Still, no one at the FBI Miami office suspected anything was wrong with Putnam, and no one there had been made aware of the Susan Smith case.

The FBI investigative team did not want to believe that Putnam was capable of committing murder, so they were careful not to expose him.

"Who's going to believe an FBI agent killed an

informant? I was astounded when I heard that," Huggins later said. "Based on Susan Smith's background, we all thought it was a bunch of nonsense at first, but when it all ended up in my lap on May 7, I told the guys I selected for this thing, you know you're investigating a fellow agent, but put that all aside, guys. Treat it just like a routine case. We're going to get to the bottom of this."

On May 16 Agent Jim Huggins, Detective Richard Ray, and Lieutenant Paul Maynard boarded an airplane in Lexington and flew down to interview Mark Putnam at the Miami FBI office. Until the interview held that day, Huggins maintained all the investigators had were allegations about Putnam's affair with Susan and his possible involvement in her disappearance. They could not accuse an FBI agent without concrete evidence, without a body, without a witness. They were still working on a missing person case, and the profile they had on Susan Smith seemed to indicate that she was capable of just running off to another state. She had done this in the past.

As Huggins readied himself for the interview with Putnam, he kept in mind that Putnam might refuse to cooperate. If that happened the case would probably remain unsolved, he knew.

But Putnam agreed to talk, and during the six and a half hour interview with Huggins and members of the KSP, the FBI man detailed his moves in Pikeville during June of 1989. Going through the three-week time period almost minute by minute, Putnam tried to itemize everything he'd done.

One of the questions Huggins asked right off

the bat was why Putnam had chosen to fly into Huntington, West Virginia, rather than Lexington, Kentucky, since he had a meeting with Tom Self in Lexington. Putnam explained that the Huntington airport was closer to Pikeville, where the chop shop trial was being held, and that answer satisfied Huggins.

Though he knew Putnam had had meetings with Self in Lexington almost every day, and landing at Lexington would probably have made more sense, Huggins said he never gave that issue a second thought. Then, when Putnam went on to explain that he was staying in Pikeville rather than Lexington because of the trial, maintaining that it was easier to travel to Lexington to see Self and then return to Pikeville for the trial, that also made sense to Agent Huggins.

"An FBI agent often drives back and forth on an official assignment. He'd think nothing of a two and a half hour trip," Huggins explained. "If Putnam had changed his lodging to Lexington, there would be a lot of paper work involved—voucher problems—and the trial was going to be held in Pikeville, so I had no problem with that."

"I tried as hard as I could to remain strictly down the line on this," Huggins said. "I didn't want to lean in his favor because he was an FBI agent. I just let him tell his story, and the story didn't completely conflict with what I knew. I didn't get the truth out of him. Not the first time."

Jim Huggins said his manner of questioning was not confrontational. He did not query Putnam sharply. A seasoned FBI man, Huggins knew he had to remain in control, had to maintain neutrality, superiority, and certainty. But he also had to be supportive, he had to keep a line of communication flowing. If Putnam was put on the defensive, he might restrict the information he provided or refuse to talk.

On May 16, 1990, Putnam denied having anything to do with Susan Smith outside of work. However, he did divulge certain information about the rental car he was driving, explaining that it had been damaged and had been turned back in. That revelation came as a surprise to Lieutenant Maynard, who had assumed that Putnam had been driving a "Bureau car" in June of 1989. Maynard had not been privy to the results of the FBI team's "homework" on the rental car.

And as the interview progressed, Putnam told his questioners something that no one in the FBI or the Kentucky State Police had known. He mentioned that he'd cut his hand on a shelf nail in the garage at his old residence in Pikeville, then said there would be blood in the rental car due to that injury. Putnam had no way of knowing whether blood had yet been discovered in the car by the FBI lab. The agent had fallen into the same trap that catches many criminals: he'd presumed the authorities knew more about his crime than they did.

But even as his story started sounding more and more deceptive, as discrepancies and new details appeared, Mark appeared relaxed, all along denying any connection with Susan Smith's disappearance.

Putnam was being too cool about the whole

matter, Agent Huggins thought. He wasn't reacting the way an innocent man should.

"If someone comes in and accuses me of murder, I'm going to be saying, Hey, you gotta be crazy! But he didn't do that. He didn't yell or get upset. He just said, 'No, I didn't do it.' "

Then, just before the interview was over, Putnam was shown the green shorts Shelby Ward had given the police. He said they were probably his, that he had a pair like them. Then he said he would let the police know whether he would take a polygraph.

On the flight back, Richard Ray sat silently, amazed that Putnam had been able to recall in such detail events, supposedly routine, that had taken place almost a year before. Like Huggins, Ray believed Putnam had been just too calm and nonchalant about being investigated as a possible murder suspect. Furthermore, instinct told him that much of Putnam's information was misleading and contrived.

"Most people don't remember what they did last week, but here Putnam was telling us things, one thing after another, about what happened back a year ago. It was branded in his brain some way. Like it was rehearsed," Ray said. "After listening to the story during that six and a half hour interview, I learned a lot that I didn't know before. I never got to talk to him after that initial time when Susan was reported missing in June of 1989. And now [after the May 16th interview], even though he was still professional and businesslike, I kind of decided that he wasn't being truthful."

On May 17, 1990, after the three lawmen returned to Lexington, Huggins made the two and a half-hour drive back to Pikeville with Paul Maynard and Richard Ray.

Later that day, they interviewed a local professional woman who claimed to be a friend of Putnam's. She said she knew Susan Smith had worked with Putnam on a bank robbery case, and she told the team that she and Putnam had spent time together from eight P.M. until three A.M. either Friday, June 9, or Saturday, June 10, 1989. But she wasn't sure which night it was.

The next day, on May 18, 1990, Huggins made a second trip down to Miami. After a brief interview, he asked Agent Putnam to make a trip with him to FBI headquarters in Washington.

"I've got a problem with two or three things you're telling me, and you're the only one that knows if you're telling the truth. I would like you to take a polygraph to satisfy me."

Even though the FBI has no legal right to force an employee to take a polygraph, it is safe to assume that refusal might have been deemed suspicious. Besides, Putnam's job was now on the line because of the repeated allegations that he had slept with a federal witness who was an FBI informant. According to Huggins, if Putnam hadn't openly admitted to the affair, an internal inquiry would have been conducted and Putnam's sexual misconduct would have been proven sooner or later, so Putnam was just days away from being removed from the Bureau in any case. "He was in serious violation of Bureau rules. His job was absolutely at stake, he should have known that," Huggins said.

The only possible source of evidence was the rental car. Putnam was informed that the FBI lab in Washington was evaluating the Ford Tempo and that it might yield traces of blood, fibers from clothing, and other evidence of foul play.

It was on the eve of Friday, May 18, that Putnam agreed to take a polygraph, and before he left Florida with Huggins, he called Kathy to tell her there might be a problem about something he had done in Pikeville. His wife was already aware of the allegation that Mark had gotten Susan pregnant, so the call didn't come as a complete surprise. But Kathy didn't believe Mark was guilty of anything. In fact, when Shelby Ward had called Terry Hulse to report the affair in June, 1989, Kathy Putnam had been infuriated that anyone might insinuate her husband was capable of such an indiscretion.

Putnam and Huggins flew to Washington, D.C., that same night, and early the next morning, Huggins escorted Putnam to FBI headquarters.

Special Agent Mark Putnam failed the polygraph.

Kentucky State Police and the FBI were angry about having been manipulated by him, but there was nothing they could do. Everything would now land in the Pike County prosecutor's lap.

When Mark returned home on the night of May 20, 1990, his wife picked him up at the airport in Fort Lauderdale at midnight, and they drove to the bar at the local Holiday Inn. It was a quiet place called David's Plum, which they had often frequented. They did not speak at all on the way there. Kathy was preparing herself for an admission of an affair with Susan Smith. She had already thought that over and had decided that she would forgive him.

When they got to their table, Mark sat in silence. Kathy ordered a double Black Russian. It came to her that he might have harmed Susan, and she wanted to get that issue cleared up right away.

"Okay, did you killer her?" she blurted out.

"Yeah, I did," Mark replied, his words not yet registering with his wife.

"You slept with her?" she asked.

"Yeah."

"This could have been your baby?"

"Yeah."

In a rage, Kathy slapped Mark so severely across the face that she knocked him out of his chair. She then downed her drink and the pair left, Mark telling her that he would have to hire an attorney first thing Monday morning.

On Monday, May 22, after contacting a lawyer in Fort Lauderdale, Putnam resigned from the FBI. That same day, Commonwealth Attorney Runyon got a call from Bruce Zimet, the lawyer Putnam had engaged.

Runyon was dumbfounded. "We had absolutely no evidence. Not one scintilla or shred. It was the first time in my twenty-eight-year career that I had a man wanting to confess to murder and I could not charge him for it," Runyon stated. He later insisted that Putnam could have gotten away with his crime if his attorney had advised him to keep his mouth shut.

"John Paul, I want to talk to you, but I need to invoke Rule Eleven of Criminal Procedure," Zimet had said the moment Runyon picked up the phone. That meant Runyon, a prosecutor, had to agree not to use anything said in the conversation in a court of law, and he did so.

"Initially Zimet talked hypothetically," Runyon later told reporters, "saying what if this had happened, what if that had happened, and finally I said, 'Look, if we're going to do this thing let's lay it on the table.' "

So Zimet started talking about manslaughter, and Runyon agreed that the facts pretty well fit that charge. It was not a cold-blooded premeditated murder, the way Zimet put it; emotion was involved. Susan Smith had backed Mark Putnam into a corner, and he had killed her during an argument, in a fit of rage.

Over a period of three weeks, Zimet and Runyon negotiated a plea bargain. During this time US Attorney Louise De Falaise and officers from the Kentucky State Police listened in on the talks, sitting in Runyon's library as Zimet's voice emanated from a speaker phone. Toward the end of the negotiations, Runyon had everyone convinced that there was no other choice but to allow Putnam to plead to manslaughter. He could not be convicted of murder without a body, and no one knew what Putnam had done with her. Susan Smith might have been hidden anywhere in Pike County.

Runyon knew he could bring in five thousand members of the Army reserve to comb the hills for a week and still not find the body of Susan Smith. Putnam knew that too. He had been around when scores of police had dug up the area for months, looking for the body of the informant Russell Davis.

Major Jerry Lovitt was also privy to the weeks of negotiations and the problems facing the Pike County prosecutor on this case. Putnam was skilled enough to cover his tracks. No one in the FBI or the local law enforcement agency could find any kind of evidence that would hold up in court. Even with an admission of manslaughter, there would be no case unless Putnam led police to Susan Smith's bones.

During the period from May 22 to June 2, 1990, Runyon kept the FBI informed on the progress of the negotiations with Zimet, and in the meanwhile, FBI agents continued their investigation. On May 24, the agents picked up copies of Susan Smith's records from the Williamson Memorial Hospital. These recorded her blood type.

That same day, Special Agent Andrew Sluss went to the *News Express* in Pikeville. Mark Putnam had stated that he had viewed *Roadhouse* at the local movie house on June 9, 1989. Sluss checked the local paper and discovered that *Roadhouse* and *Pink Cadillac* were showing until June 8, 1989. On June 9, the movies had switched to *Final Frontier,* and *See No Evil.*

On June 1, Agents Sam Smith and Tim Adams went to Putnam's former residence on Honeysuckle Drive and inspected the shelves and paint cans in what used to be Putnam's garage. They were told by the home's new owner, Mrs. Bolton, that the shelves had remained untouched since she had moved into the house. The FBI agents found no nails or sharp objects on them that would cut a hand, nor could they locate any blood splatters around the shelf area.

Meanwhile, the negotiations between Runyon and Zimet were becoming heated. Zimet called at one point and said Putnam would take twelve years. Runyon said he would take no less than sixteen and hung up.

"We selectively analyzed this thing," Runyon said. "I did the plea bargaining, and I told Mr. Putnam's attorney, on the telephone, that I couldn't sleep with less than sixteen years—I tell you, we were taking bets that Putnam would back out, but he didn't."

The bargaining went back and forth for days until Zimet called back and finally agreed to the sixteen-year plea bargain.

On June 4, 1990, Special Agent Jim Huggins and Lieutenant Paul Maynard flew down to Miami to witness the statement Putnam was to make in the presence of his attorney. This sworn confession would later be used in the court case against him.

By the time they got to Zimet's Ford Lauderdale office, it was already beginning to grow dark outside. At eight P.M. Huggins asked Putnam to disclose the whereabouts of Susan Smith's body before he made his confession, so that FBI agents and Kentucky State Police could locate her. Putnam said he had "placed" Susan Smith down a ravine off Harmon's Branch, just nine miles outside Pikeville, and he described the exact location where the body could be found. Paul Maynard went into the next room and called the Pikeville post, at which FBI agents and Kentucky State Police were standing by for directions which would lead them to Susan Smith's remains.

At eight forty-five P.M., FBI agents Smith and Adams, accompanied by State Police Sergeant Fred Davidson and his search dog, Bingo, arrived at Harmon's Branch and drove up the steep, windy dirt road. Unfortunately, the area where Susan Smith was supposed to have been placed was so heavily overgrown, they could not locate any trace of a corpse. Their bloodhound, Bingo, sniffed around for some time, picking up no scent.

The team searched the area for a full fifteen minutes, standing in the exact location Maynard had given them. They had drawn a map, pinpointing the spot. Despite their specific instructions as to where the body of Susan Smith was, they couldn't find it. The men, who had gone down over the steep embankment beside the road and into the ravine, were now so covered by trees and brambles, they were hardly visible to the officers on guard above. Bingo, the search dog, could not be seen as he wandered aimlessly in the impenetrable woods.

Just before nightfall, one of the men spotted what he thought was a skull. Down among the briars, the team now uncovered a human skeleton, the rib cage intact, partially concealed by leaves, the arm and leg bones seemingly shifted around, perhaps by wild animals. One of the men picked up the jawbone. It was missing two molar teeth. No flesh was visible on any of the bones, and the body, which appeared to have been thrown or dropped over the edge of the ravine, had rolled or slid until coming up against an old fence that had been heaved down the slope earlier. There were no articles of clothing at the site.

State troopers were left on guard at Harmon's Branch until the forensic anthropologist, Dr. David Wolfe, arrived from Frankfort.

A gold chain and cross lying next to the skeleton were later identified as jewelry Shelby had lent Susan. This was the only item which positively identified the remains as being those of Susan Daniels Smith.

Back in Fort Lauderdale, on June 4, 1990, Mark Steven Putnam confessed to killing Susan Daniels Smith, becoming the first agent in the eighty-two-year history of the FBI to be charged in a homicide-related offense.

Having been advised of his constitutional rights by Senior Special Agent Huggins, Putnam began reading his sworn statement aloud to Huggins and Maynard. The confession addressed previous statements he had made regarding the disappearance of Susan Smith. These had contained some false information, and Putnam declared, "I now wish to tell the complete truth regarding this matter."

In accordance with the plea agreement between Putnam and Runyon, the former FBI agent furnished this statement based on assurances that he would not be prosecuted for any false statements he'd made relative to the investigation, and he claimed that prior to Susan's death, he was "feeling a lot of pressure because of the upcoming trial, the move to Miami, and the constant badgering by Susan over her pregnancy." All of these were factors that led to his act of uncontrolled rage, Putnam revealed.

In his sworn confession, he said he'd attempted to discuss Susan's pregnancy with her on several occasions and he'd informed her that once the baby was born, he would take a blood test to determine whether he was in fact the father. But Susan only became hostile and antagonistic whenever the subject was raised. He added that on several occasions he attempted to discuss Susan's pregnancy with her, and he said he specifically recalled asking Susan whether she should consider an abortion or his providing for the child by adopting the child, but she would entertain neither idea.

According to Putnam's version of the killing, at about seven P.M. on June 8, 1989, he arrived in Pikeville, having just returned from Lexington where he was working on pretrial matters with Assistant United States Attorney Tom Self. He was driving a blue Ford Tempo, a rented car. At approximately eight-thirty P.M. Susan Smith had started calling his room to complain about his not meeting with her to discuss her pregnancy, and to accuse him of being the father of her child. Then at ten-thirty P.M., Susan went to his room, where she became more vocal and argumentative. Putnam said he told her to "shut up," and they got into a loud argument. Then he began to fear that other people staying at the motel might overhear their bickering, and he asked Susan to go for a ride with him so they could continue the discussion.

When they got into Putnam's rental car, they drove around the Pikeville area and then headed out into the eastern end of Pike County, in the vicinity of Phelps.

"All during the drive, we discussed the pregnancy issue and I kept asking Susan what she wanted me to do," Putnam stated. "She would never give me a specific answer, but kept telling me the baby was mine and she was going to 'hang me' over that. She said she would tell the FBI, my family, and the newspapers. I was getting extremely uptight."

The argument continued, and at approximately midnight, Putnam claims he parked his car near the top of Peter Creek Mountain, not far from Susan's home. At that point in their conversation, he told her that he and his wife Kathy would adopt the baby if it was his, saying he could give the baby a much better home than she could.

"I told her that if custody were to be decided in court, the court would definitely rule in my favor because of her background," Putnam admitted, adding that Susan then became enraged and he, in an act of anger, slammed his right hand "into the dashboard or the console," cutting it so it bled.

"At this time Susan started striking me with her hands in a slapping-type motion," Putnam continued. "And in an act of extreme rage, I reached across the car and grabbed her by the throat with both hands. I straddled her, actually sitting on top of her in the seat."

Putnam said he then started choking Susan, again telling her to "shut up." He estimated that he choked her for approximately two minutes, during which time "Susan continued to struggle and strike me about the face." During this struggle, Putnam guessed that Susan's feet were positioned against the passenger-side windshield, which he later noticed was cracked. "I believed she had done this during the struggle," he asserted.

After Susan ceased struggling, Putnam relaxed his grip, assuming she was unconscious. He then checked for a pulse, and finding none, he began to administer mouth-to-mouth resuscitation techniques. He even took his fist and hit her chest in an attempt to get her breathing again, but with no success. Susan did not move.

In a state of panic, Putnam exited by the door on the driver's side and removed Susan from the passenger side of the vehicle. He said he was feeling faint and she "felt extremely heavy to me." He sat her on the ground, propping her up against his legs, but when he released his grip, she fell to the side, her head striking the ground with a "thud." At this point, Putnam said, he decided that Susan was dead.

"Realizing she was wearing my clothing, which was a pair of gray casual shorts with two long pockets in the front and a gray pullover gym shirt I had given her earlier in the week, I removed the clothing from her body," Putnam said. He told police that he later disposed of the items in a trash receptacle at the Landmark Inn.

Putnam then placed Susan's body in the trunk of the rental car and drove back to the Landmark Inn in Pikeville. It was approximately two-thirty A.M. when he parked in the lot. He went directly to his room and took a shower. He then went to the Super America Market, located across the street from the Landmark, and purchased some Band-Aids and medicine to apply to his hand. When he returned to his room he was "extremely scared and nervous and did not know what to do."

Putnam maintained that he sat up for the rest of the night, and then at six-thirty or seven A.M., after taking another shower, he departed for Lexington to meet with Tom Self for a pretrial conference. Susan's body remained in the trunk during this time, Putnam said, and upon his arrival in Lexington, he parked the rental car in front of the Lexington courthouse, where it remained for the rest of the day.

According to his statement, Putnam said he left Lexington at about five P.M., arriving in Pikeville around seven P.M. at which time he went to McDonald's and had something to drink. He then started the grim journey to dispose of the body.

He proceeded north on US 23 to Harmon's Branch Road, nine miles outside of Pikeville, and after driving a short distance on Harmon's Branch, Putnam found a turnoff at the left side of the road. He backed his vehicle into it and removed Susan's body from the trunk.

"I then proceeded to place the body in a small

ravine and laid Susan on her back," Putnam stated, adding, "There were some weeds and undergrowth, and I thought someone would find her." Susan was nude, and after he had put her down, Putnam said he sat beside her for a minute and then "kissed her on the cheek."

Before he got to the top of the mountain, Putnam said he passed a man who looked at him very closely. The man was standing in his yard and appeared to be in his fifties. Putnam stated that while he was placing Susan's body in the ravine, he'd heard dirt bikes in the area, and that when he got back into his car and sat there for a few minutes, he observed a girl riding by on a horse. She'd looked at him and ridden on.

He left Harmon's Branch and went back to the Landmark, certain that "Susan's body would be found in a short period of time."

Later that evening, Putnam said, he called his wife and was so tired that he "went to sleep during the conversation."

He swore that he was not aware of any witnesses to his and Susan's departure from the Landmark on June 8, and he further stated that he did not have his weapon with him when he left the motel and he did not shoot Susan. He added that Susan did not have any type of weapon with her.

"At the time of the altercation," Putnam continued, "neither Susan nor I were under the influence of any drugs or alcohol. No other person was aware of, nor did anyone else participate in, the death of Susan Smith. Also, I never told anyone else about the particulars of Susan's death and I never returned to the location of the body."

Putnam then admitted to first having sexual intercourse with Susan Smith in December, 1988. From that time until the time of her death, he said he had had intercourse with her "approximately four to five times." He admitted the baby Susan was carrying at the time of her death could have been his child, because "I never used birth control during intercourse with Susan."

Putnam claimed that Susan never mentioned a previous pregnancy or miscarriage to him. He further stated that the times he had had sex with her, it was always in the car, never at his house or at a motel, and he denied having sexual relations with her during the days prior to her death. He insisted that he was trying to avoid her that entire week.

Putnam then retracted an earlier statement he had made to investigators regarding Susan's meeting with a group from Illinois on a drug deal, stating that it was false information.

In the remainder of his confession, Putnam told law enforcement how he went about cleaning up the scene of the crime, explaining that on Saturday, June 10, 1989, after he went to serve a subpoena in the nearby town of Salyersville, Kentucky, he returned to Pikeville at about ten A.M. and went to the One Stop Car Wash, where he vacuumed out the rental car. While he was cleaning it out, he noticed an earring "of which I did not know the origin," so he vacuumed it up. Putnam also bought some liquid cleaner and water, and removed the blood from the interior of the vehicle.

Also on Saturday—Putnam said he could not

recall the exact time — he removed the mat from the trunk of the car and discarded it on the microwave-tower access road, adjacent to the jogging track at the Bob Amos Park in Pikeville. He did that, Putnam said, because when he took Susan's body out of the trunk to place it in the ravine, he noticed some human "discharge" on the mat, "apparently from Susan's mouth."

Sometime in the afternoon on that Saturday, Putnam claimed, he drove to his old neighborhood on Honeysuckle Drive, stopping by his former residence and then visiting Celia Fish, who had been his neighbor. Putnam stated that one of Celia's children noticed a cut on his hand, and he explained to the child that he had injured it on a nail in his garage. Fish, a registered nurse, later told police that she did see Putnam that evening, but neither she nor her children noticed a bandage or cut on either of Putnam's hands.

It was well into the evening on June 4, 1990, when Putnam finally finished his statement, calmly stating that he had returned to the Landmark the evening after the killing and was engaged in trial activities in Pikeville until June 25, 1989, at which time he departed for Miami.

"Putnam's confession was orchestrated," Major Lovitt of the KSP said in retrospect. "Putnam was playing out his hand of cards, and he did it very skillfully. He knew exactly what the system's weaknesses were.

"He knew there was some pressure to solve this case. He knew we didn't have a damn thing on him, and he knew what cards we had, so there was no

bluffing. We couldn't use any of the usual lines.
. . . Intimidation was taken out of our hands and
put into his. Then he ran us back and forth to Miami two and three times. We were thinking this guy
is crooked, he's a law officer, he's killed a person,
and he's not going to get away with that."

Chapter Fourteen

On the morning of June 5, 1990, forensic anthropologist Dr. David Wolfe, a man with a national reputation, who had handled hundreds of excavations, appeared at Harmon's Branch to collect Susan Smith's remains: the larger bones, a few bright red fingernails and other small human fragments, some stray teeth, some pieces of cartilage, all of which were gathered as evidence and put into small plastic containers. Wolfe continued to dig through dry leaves and earth, uncovering most of Smith's bones, only two of which were later discovered to be missing, possibly having been carried off by animals. As members of the Kentucky State Police looked on and took photographs, the anthropologist carefully placed Susan Smith's remains, along with a great mass of earth, into eight twelve-gallon buckets.

At the time of the discovery, an unidentified coal-mine employee told David Wolfe that he had smelled something horrible around the site a year before, but, thinking the stench came from some dead animal, he'd never gotten out of his mechanized cart to check on what lay over the hill. The man told Wolfe the smell ceased after a few days, and he thought no more about it.

Another coal worker who appeared at the excavation site explained to Wolfe that the coal company had already made plans to fill in the entire area with cement, and Susan Smith would have been buried forever if the police had taken any longer to find her. Those plans fell through, however, and Harmon's Branch remains a remote dirt road.

Before David Wolfe left the area with Smith's remains, he promised the Pike county coroner some answers regarding Susan Smith's death, and he drove back to Frankfort, where he began the postmortem exam.

Meanwhile, two FBI agents, William Welsh and Tommy Gayheart, were assigned to search for the trunk mat of the 1989 Ford Tempo Putnam had driven on the night of the murder. The agents were assisted by three officers in searching the Bob Amos Park area, using long sticks to beat the weeds at the jogging track. They were not able to locate the liner.

Later that same day, Putnam's statement was presented to the Commonwealth Attorney and Runyon immediately had his secretary get Shelby Ward on the phone.

"Can you be at my office at nine tomorrow morning?" Runyon asked her politely.

"Susan's dead isn't she?" Shelby asked.

"I'm afraid so," Runyon said.

"What happened to her?"

But Runyon wouldn't give Shelby any more details over the phone, so she hung up and began screaming, tears flowing down her cheeks. Since Ike Ward was away at an auction, she called her brother, Bo, and asked him to come spend the night with her. She said she was afraid to be alone.

"They wouldn't tell me where they found her or if there was anything of her left, they wouldn't tell me a thing," Shelby shrieked over the phone.

"Well, you know they're all a bunch of damn liars. They've been covering this thing up for a year now, Shelb. They've probably known about Suzie all along," Bo responded in a choked voice.

That night neither Shelby nor Billy Joe could sleep. Shelby was crying all night long, and her brother was trying to console her, to no avail. The two of them decided not to inform anyone else in the family that Susan's remains had been found, not until they had more details.

They surmised that Mark Putnam had murdered Susan, but they had no concrete answers yet. All along, they had held on to the possibility that Susan was alive somewhere, under witness protection. Now that hope had ended. Still, the idea that Susan was never coming back seemed unreal to them.

By six A.M. Shelby and Billy Joe were already dressed and ready to go to Pikeville. They got to Runyon's office at exactly nine A.M., but were asked to sit in the lobby, where they waited for over an hour. During that time, Shelby could hear Runyon, behind the closed door, talking on the phone. His voice was muffled, but she could make out the name Putnam. Runyon repeated it over and over.

"He's killed her, Bo," Shelby said to her brother in a choked voice.

"Well, we don't know that for sure yet," Bo told her.

"You can hear him talking on the phone, can't you?" Shelby whispered. "Don't you hear him saying 'Putnam'?"

Finally, Shelby and Billy Joe were called into Runyon's office. Shelby remembers that what struck her at the time was Runyon's blank expression. She claims the prosecutor showed no compassion or remorse, not any. "Like Susan was nothing," she said. Special Agent Terry O'Conner was in the office, and Shelby recalls his hand was shaking as he told her, "We want to apologize of behalf of the agency for what has happened to your sister."

"Mark killed her, didn't he?" Shelby blurted out.

"I'm afraid so," Runyon responded.

"How was she killed?" Shelby asked.

"Strangulation. He strangled her to death. We have a full confession from him. Mark's got a lawyer; his name is Bruce Zimet. Mark wanted to confess about killing Susan. He told us where the body was, over on Harmon's Branch here right outside Pikeville, and we went and got it the day before yesterday."

"Well, where is the body now? Is there anything left of her?" Shelby wanted to know.

"Just skeletal remains," Runyon said, and then, after a moment of silence, he added, "Putnam and his lawyer worked out a plea agreement with me for a sixteen-year sentence."

"Only sixteen years, John Paul?" Shelby was shocked.

"That was the best deal we could get."

"Well, that's not a very long time to give a man who killed two people," she quipped.

"In the state of Kentucky, it's not considered murder if the baby's not born — even if the woman is nine months pregnant, there's no provision for murder in the case of an unborn fetus."

"He murdered my sister in cold blood. I want him to get the death penalty," Shelby shouted.

"The facts in this case pretty well fit manslaughter, Shelby. If you look at the confession, you'll see what I'm talking about," Runyon insisted.

"I don't care about any confession. My sister was left to lay over the hill there for a year, like a dog! Putnam's getting away with murder!"

"Shelby, when they called here, they started out with just six years, and I said no way. Then they came up to twelve years, and I hung up the phone on them. But when they came back with sixteen years, I said I'd take it, because we had nothing to convict the man on without his confession, and you can't expect Putnam to take the maximum penalty when he never would have been charged unless he cooperated with us."

"It was murder! Cold-blooded murder!" Bo raged.

"The way it happened, it fits a manslaughter plea. I want you both to look over the confession. Then it might make more sense to you."

"You sound like you're upholding Mark!" Shelby cried.

"We couldn't have ever gotten him if it hadn't happened this way. All we had to go by was the lie detector test, and they aren't admissible in court. We never would have found the body unless we made a plea bargain where he would confess and lead us to her. Without a body, there was no way to prove a crime. We could have combed the hills of Pike County for months and have never found her body."

"Are we going to have a trial?" Shelby asked.

"No. We don't go to trial when there's a plea bargain. We're having him brought in on June twelfth at nine A.M. We need you two to be here on the tenth at nine A.M. to meet with members of the Grand Jury. They will hear your testimony. I'm sorry this had to happen to your sister," Runyon said in a flat tone.

Shelby and Bo left Runyon's office in a daze. They couldn't understand why they hadn't been consulted about the plea agreement. They couldn't believe that the Commonwealth could let a man get away with murder by calling it manslaughter. Outraged, they now had to go back to Freeburn to face their relatives and explain what had happened. Then there were Susan's two small children. They had to be told the horrible truth.

The news tore the family to pieces, and for a few days, everyone was in a state of shock. There was still no word about burial or about the results of the autopsy. For the time being, only the sentencing of Mark Putnam had to be dealt with.

Early in the morning on June 10, Shelby and her brother went back to Pikeville to meet with the Grand Jury. She was chain smoking out in the hallway before she walked into the Grand Jury room, pacing the floor while John Paul Runyon was inside talking for what seemed an hour. When he would periodically come into the hallway, Shelby would grab him and say, "When am I going to get to go in there?" But Runyon just put her off, saying "In a little while" every time he walked by her.

When Shelby Ward finally went before the Grand Jury, she says she felt like she was the one on trial. She couldn't believe the way the jury members stared at her. It appeared to her that every one of them was scared.

"Do you promise to tell the truth, the whole truth, and nothing but the truth, so help you God?" an official asked her. Shelby said, "Yes," then sat down on her isolated chair.

The first thing John Paul Runyon did in front of the jury was explain to her that if they didn't go ahead with this plea bargain, if they took the case to court, if they took it to trial, Mark Putnam would walk out a free man, Shelby stated.

"Well, I don't understand that. Putnam is a cold-blooded murderer," she had protested.

"All I can say is, if we don't go with this deal we've got, we're going to blow the whole thing," Runyon said. "Do you remember coming into my office in February and talking to me?"

"Yes, John Paul."

"Well, we had nothing then, and if it hadn't been for the FBI getting involved, and for my negotiations, there wouldn't have been any confession."

Runyon laid everything out for Shelby. He read the confession and the plea. She felt she couldn't interrupt, but before she left the stand, she was asked if there was anything she would like to tell the jury. Her statement was limited to five minutes.

"Mark and Susan had a love affair, Mark got her pregnant, and then he kills her, and I think it shouldn't be this deal that John Paul's worked out. Him being down there and living the good life down in Florida for a whole year, living it up, the whole time knowing that we were going crazy looking for Susan," Shelby protested. "I don't want you to go along with this deal. I want to have him tried for cold-blooded murder and give him the maximum sentence. I want him to have two life sentences! He killed his unborn child!"

"That's all we need Shelby, thank you. You can go now," Runyon said, and he shuffled her out of the room.

"Runyon practically shoved me out the door," Shelby recalls. "I had to beg him to let my brother Billy Joe get in there and talk to the Grand Jury. After Bo tells them about the affair and the trips to Pikeville and everything, John Paul asks him if there was anything he wanted to add, and all Bo got out was one grunt before John Paul says, 'Well, that will be all, thank you.'"

According to the Pike Circuit Court documents, Commonwealth Attorney Runyon made the members of the Grand Jury aware of the various constraints and legal principles placed upon the investigating law officers and prosecutors. One of these was the Fifth Amendment of the United States Constitution, which provides that no person can be compelled to testify against himself or in any way give evidence that would place him in jeopardy.

The Grand Jury was further advised that these plea negotiations were entered into under the constraints imposed by Rule Eleven of the Criminal Rules of Procedure.

Although Mark Steven Putnam had the motive and the opportunity to kill Susan Daniels Smith, and although circumstantial evidence indicated that he had, in fact, killed her, there were no eye witnesses, and there was no physical evidence to support a criminal charge. Prior to his confession, no homicide charge could have been supported because no body had been found, the jury members were told.

The Grand Jury was further informed that the results of a lie detector test were inadmissible in court, and for that reason, a decision had been made to enter into negotiations with Putnam through his attorney. As a result of the negotations carried out by Runyon, Putnam, and Zimet, Mark Putnam had agreed to admit his involvement in Susan Smith's disappearance and to provide details.

The twelve people listened carefully as Runyon explained that in return for a complete disclosure of the location of the body of Susan Smith and of the manner in which she died, the Commonwealth agreed to recommend a sixteen-year term of imprisonment if Putnam pleaded guilty to first-degree manslaughter. The Grand Jury then had the opportunity to discuss the case and review the statement by Putnam, as well as the plea agreement signed by the parties involved. With one man's dissent—Martin Luther Johnson of Pikeville refused to comply—the Grand Jury recommended that the plea agreement be ratified and accepted by the court.

Putnam's confession had managed to satisfy the FBI, the Kentucky State Police, and the Pike County prosecutor. All agreed that the murder was not premeditated, and when the nine-page confession was presented to the Grand Jury in Pikeville on June 11, the panel of citizens saw no alternative but to return an indictment of manslaughter.

The general consensus was that without the help of Mark Putnam, the body of Susan Smith would probably never have been found and the case would never have been solved. It was the opinion of the Grand Jury that the charge of manslaughter and the recommendation of sixteen years in prison reflected the realities of the case.

Once the jury had agreed to the plea bargain, they told the court that they felt justice would be served in two ways: first, the family of Susan Smith could begin to adjust and to reconstruct their lives now that they knew her fate; and second, a guilty man would be punished for his crime. The indictment was handed down on June 12, 1990, minutes before Mark Steven Putnam appeared in the Pike County Circuit court for an open arraignment.

The small Pike County courthouse was packed

and feelings ran high on June 12 when Putnam was to be brought in and sentenced. Before he entered the room, Shelby Ward set off the metal detector and was detained for carrying a gun in her purse. The weapon was wrapped in a sock — and loaded. Shelby claimed she had just forgotten about it. "I wasn't going to shoot him," she later insisted. Police confiscated the gun and let Shelby proceed into the courtroom, escorted and guarded by members of the Kentucky State Police. She received a written citation upon leaving the courtroom and had to face John Paul Runyon on a weapons charge.

As everyone waited for Mark Putnam's appearance, the atmosphere became more tense. TV and newspaper reporters filled one side of the courtroom, adding to the air of excitement, but Billy Joe Daniels was the only other member of Susan's family besides Shelby in the courtroom that day, her parents and children being too distressed to attend.

Of course there was little doubt as to what was going to transpire once Putnam appeared. Everything had been prearranged between the attorneys and agreed to by the Grand Jury. Putnam was going to walk away with a sixteen-year sentence. He was mandated to serve only half of that. After eight years he would become eligible for parole.

Judge Baird Collier, who pronounced sentence, later explained that he had only two options with regard to the plea agreement drawn up by Runyon and Putnam's attorney once the indictment had been returned.

"You either accept the plea as agreed by the

Commonwealth Attorney and the defendant, or you tell the defendant, I will not accept the plea," Collier said. "I could have rejected the plea but I didn't because the Grand Jury report indicated that if the plea were rejected, nothing that the police had gained from Mr. Putnam's testimony would ever again be admissible against him. That was part of the agreement between Putnam and the Commonwealth Attorney."

In Judge Collier's opinion, if he rejected Putnam's plea, he wouldn't have been able to charge Putnam with anything, since contained within the plea agreement was a document which stipulated that if the plea was rejected, Putnam would then enter a "not guilty" plea and would be able to sign his own bond. In that case, he would have been able to walk out of the courtroom a free man.

Judge Collier was put into an awkward spot. "It was the only information I had before me. It's a believable story. I obviously do not know what happened . . . I feel as though, with the facts presented to me, I went with the only alternative I saw. I think that if you had a hundred circuit judges, and they were put into the position that I was put into, they would have done the same thing."

Mark Steven Putnam's climactic court appearance on June 12, 1990, lasted less than an hour.

He walked into the courtroom wearing a white button-down shirt, blue jeans, and high-top sneakers, entering by the back door, behind the judge's chair. Bruce Zimet was on his right, and a police officer was on his left. Putnam's knees gave out as he passed through the doorway, and his attorney had to hold him up, grabbing him tightly by the arm as he led him to his seat.

Putnam's confession was attached to the Pike County Grand Jury indictment, and as soon as the judge handed down the indictment, John Paul Runyon made a motion to seal it until the arraignment. Shelby Ward and Billy Joe Daniels stared at Putnam, but the former FBI man refused to look at them, keeping his head down. The courtroom was packed with policemen, people from the media, and the curious. The overflow filled the foyer, but neither Kathy Putnam nor Ron Poole was present.

Putnam refused to look at the cameras or at the other people in the room, keeping his hands over his face much of the time; and before the judge spoke, Shelby said, "You could hear a pin drop."

Then Judge Collier told Putnam to approach the bench.

"At this time, are you under any emotional stress?" Collier asked.

"No, sir," Putnam said.

"On June 8, 1989, did you take Susan Daniels Smith's life?" Collier asked.

"Yes, sir, I did," Putnam unequivocally stated.

After a string of technical questions, to which Putnam repeatedly answered yes, Collier pronounced sentence.

"The court finds that the defendant understands the nature of the charge against him . . . that there is a factual basis for the defendant's plea. . . . It is therefore ordered that the defendant is guilty of the offense of First-Degree Manslaughter and the court notes the Commonwealth's recommendation of sixteen years in the penitentiary."

Although murder or manslaughter is a state crime, not a federal offense, Putnam did not wind up in a state penitentiary, but in the federal correctional facility in Otisville, New York. Because it was agreed in the plea bargain between Zimet and Runyon that Putnam, for his safety, would not be retained in the state's custody, Runyon had made arrangements through the State Corruptions Cabinet to have Putnam incarcerated in another state, in a federal facility.

The Kentucky State Police escorted Putnam, in handcuffs, to the Lexington airport, from which he was transported to New York. During the trip to Lexington, Putnam told KSP Detective Claude Tackett that he took the body to three locations before choosing Harmon's Branch. Putnam said he first went up Island Creek in Pikeville, near a firing range, then passed the range, traveling on a dirt roadway near the top of the mountain. Putnam had not liked this location because he'd felt the body might not have been found. He had then gone to the Bob Amos Park, also on top of a hill, but again he'd had a feeling Susan's body wouldn't be found there.

Back in Pikeville, the media swarmed out on the courthouse steps, asking Susan Smith's brother and sister to comment on the outcome of the unusual case.

"It might have taken some time, but I think we could have gotten a murder conviction on it," Billy Joe Daniels told the local TV reporters. "I want a new prosecutor on the thing, not any plea bargain," he stated, and Shelby Ward chimed in, telling reporters that Runyon hadn't informed her about the negotiations, that she hadn't had a chance to agree or disagree to anything, and asserting that she'd been mistreated by Runyon, the FBI, and the Kentucky State Police throughout the entire investigation.

"This is the dirtiest county I've ever seen in my life," Shelby said, looking into the TV cameras. "I think they're covering everything up." Shelby then told the press that when she called Terry Hulse, the FBI supervisor in Louisville, Hulse had brushed her off. "He talked to me like Susan didn't need to be looked for," she said.

Hulse had already become the subject of an internal FBI investigation and was not allowed to discuss the case. Poole, also under FBI scrutiny, refused any interviews, but called Shelby twice after Putnam's trial.

Terry O'Conner, the head of the FBI in Kentucky, called the Putnam sentencing "a difficult day," and he told TV news reporters that he hoped "the entire record of the FBI would be what governs the way people think about the agency." O'Conner denied that Putnam had received preferential treatment because of his status as an agent and added, "The matter will become the subject of an internal FBI investigation to determine whether there are any administrative steps that need to be taken or any procedures that need to be tightened up."

In the meantime, outside the courtroom, Runyon held his first press conference in his twenty-eight years as a prosecutor. He defended the plea bargain, telling reporters, "Justice, like beauty, is in the eye of the beholder." Runyon said he believed Putnam confessed "because of his conscience and his hope to save his soul." Even though the Commonwealth Attorney met with harsh criticism from Susan Smith's family and members of the press, he repeatedly told reporters that he would have agreed to the same plea bargain if the defendant had been an unemployed coal miner.

In New England, the minister of the church Putnam's father had attended, Bruce Johnson of Coventry, was contacted by Mark's mother, who asked him to visit Mark in Otisville, New York, at the correctional facility where her son was being held temporarily. Johnson went to the jail and spent about fifteen minutes with the former FBI agent, during which time the two men sat in a private room, Putnam displaying his shame and remorse over the incident. Putnam had no handcuffs on, and Johnson said the prison was "secured" for Putnam's protection.

"Putnam was led to the visiting area down special corridors so that other prisoners would not catch sight of him," Johnson recalled. "They made sure he wouldn't be passing through populated areas when they brought him from his cell.

"My role was to see him, talk to him, and determine that he was okay," Johnson explained. "There was a guard with us the whole time Mark and I talked. Afterwards I went back to his family and told them Mark was all right. The Putnams were making arrangements to go see him while he was there in Otisville."

Mark's brother, Tim Putnam, an employee of the Connecticut legislature, later told the Associated Press that the case had made life painful for everyone. "I see a lot of people we both grew up with. They're all shocked, because it's not something you'd expect of Mark or anyone in our family."

Tim Putnam told reporters that his brother hadn't called him from jail, explaining, "I think he's embarrassed. Not really proud about what he did or where he is."

Then there was also the shocked reaction of those people who personally knew Mark, his friends and neighbors, none of whom could believe that he committed such a heinous act.

"My first reaction was to bust out laughing," Pikeville resident Mark Sohn told reporters, "I just didn't think it was true."

"He's always been extraordinarily kind, considerate, and nice," Charles Edwards exclaimed. Edwards was a friend of Putnam's from a neighboring eastern Kentucky county. "This had to have been an explosive situation."

When Putnam's former soccer coach and his old teammates were questioned by reporters in Tampa, they were equally stunned.

"No way," insisted Michael Fall, a teammate at Tampa, when he was told about the killing. "It's totally the opposite of what he was."

"There must have been some extreme extenuating circumstances that pushed him over the edge," said his former Tampa soccer coach, Jay Miller. "This had to have been a work-related involvement. Putnam must have gotten so involved in some case, he got tangled up with this girl."

Police officers in West Virginia were also shocked. Roby Pope told reporters it gave him the cold chills to hear about it. "Mark was the last guy in the world that I'd have thought would do something like that," Pope said. He couldn't believe Putnam had broken the golden rule and become involved with Susan Smith. "Personal involvement with an informant — that's a cardinal sin," he declared.

Then, just about the time the press got word of Putnam being in a New York facility, he was transferred to a permanent correctional institution in Rochester, Minnesota. Kathy Putnam moved up there with her two children, wanting to be near the man she still loved. She later told a reporter that she and the kids were visiting the prison regularly, that Putnam's release date had been set for January 12, 2002.

Back in Kentucky, the story of Susan Daniels Smith made front-page headlines for days, with reporters blaming the FBI and the Kentucky State Police for not investigating Agent Mark Putnam sooner. Runyon's position that he had bargained with Putnam because the police investigation had not uncovered enough evidence was attacked, reporters claiming that the state police case file and the interviews with witnesses suggested the authorities might have been able to build a case against Putnam if they had reacted quickly, instead of letting eight months elapse before they decided to pursue the former FBI agent.

The plea bargain now became a controversial public matter. Editorials sprang up, condemning the FBI for almost letting one of their own get away with murder. State Police investigators were condemned for ignoring FBI Agent Mark Putnam as a suspect. Of course the biggest question was: why did it take police eight months to focus on FBI Agent Mark Putnam as a prime suspect? The fact that the FBI didn't investigate Putnam, even though his supervisor was aware of the allegations against him early on, was deemed inexcusable by the press and by the public.

Letters to the editor recommended a "housecleaning" of the justice system, accused the FBI of "an underhanded cover-up," and attacked the prosecutor for "selling out his public trust." Mark Putnam's plea of manslaughter was called "criminal."

One letter in the *Lexington Herald Leader* condemned the whole law enforcement system for allowing one of its own to "get off light," insisting that the facts indicated this was a case of murder, not manslaughter. "This was not a simple passion killing," the outraged man wrote. "Agent Putnam threw Susan Daniels Smith's naked body, with her unborn child, into the garbage dump, to rot like table scraps. This was more than an illegal abortion that large numbers of the public are calling murder. It was a cold-blooded murder and a cover-up, with a transfer to Miami, away from the scene of the crime."

Gary Johnson, an appellate attorney with the Kentucky public defender's office, told a reporter that the ten FBI agents who were sent to Pike County "had sophisticated methods that could have been used to solve the case without a confession." Of course Runyon responded to Johnson's criticism calling it "totally imaginative." But Johnson, voicing the opinion of many of the people of the region, insisted to Kentucky newspapermen that, had this been anyone but a poor girl from a hollow in Pike County, it would have been entirely different."

Anthony Bouza, a former police chief from the Bronx in New York City, was quoted in *The Lexington Herald Leader* as saying, "Kentucky State police lost valuable time by not going after Putnam sooner. . . . These cases are highly perishable, and the longer they're let go, the harder they get to solve. . . . There was plenty of physical evidence they could have developed. The record should at least be reflective of a more sincere and thoroughgoing effort."

James Starrs, a professor of criminal science at George Washington University in D.C., also accused law enforcement of doing a poor job. Starrs pointed out that police did not conduct a laboratory examination of the motel room where Smith stayed or of the belongings she left behind. He also mentioned that police failed to quickly locate Putnam's rental car and check it out, and they didn't immediately get an accounting of where he was, and with whom, at the time of Susan Smith's disappearance.

"I think this is a gross example of the gross underemployment of the forensic sciences and the investigative tools available to the police," Starrs told reporters, "probably caused by the fact that he was a law enforcement agent with whom they had worked."

George Parry, former head of special investigations for the Philadelphia district attorney, told reporters that he would have focused the investigation on Putnam sooner, and blasted the FBI for allowing Ron Poole to unofficially investigate Smith's disappearance, stating, "the FBI immediately should have sent in independent investigators to clean up what was obviously a problem office."

Again and again, the FBI was attacked by newspapers for having known about the affair and the pregnancy and for refusing to investigate Putnam themselves. The general impression was that the delay in pursuing Putnam indicated law enforcement personnel, particularly those in the FBI, had closed ranks to protect one of their own.

Special Agent Jim Huggins, in charge of the Putnam investigation, was furious about this negative press, later saying, "That was the thing that bothered me more than anything . . . We got involved in this thing May 7, and we did an outstanding piece of work. Myself and the other agents, we all went into this with heart and soul, and found her body within four or five weeks . . . he was convicted, he was sentenced. I feel good about that."

And in response to the whirlwind of bad press, Terry O'Conner, special agent in charge in Louisville, publicly defended the FBI's efforts, assuring people in a newspaper editorial that the internal inquiry into the matter would "put an end to questions of inappropriate behaviors or practices of FBI officials." O'Conner then commended the FBI in undertaking the case of Susan Daniels Smith as a kidnapping investigation.

When another newspaper editorial appeared, this one calling for State Attorney General Fred Cowan to appoint an independent counsel to investigate the state police's handling of the investigation, Kentucky's top state police official, Justice Secretary W. Michael Troop, held a news conference to defend the investigation of Susan Smith's slaying.

"I'm not going to stand by and let the integrity and honesty of the Kentucky State Police be attacked," Troop told reporters. "The editorial in the paper wanted to know how the KSP reacted when an FBI agent turned killer. I can tell you how we reacted. We sent him to jail. I'm not going to engage in Monday morning quarterbacking when I can see what the end result was."

State Police Major Jerry Lovitt called a news conference and told reporters, "The evidence against Putnam amounted to hearsay." He added that even if a love affair had been going on, "there was no reason for us to believe that she had been murdered." Lovitt said Putnam was not a suspect because state police were treating Susan Smith as a missing person case. Lovitt complimented the police for their diligent investigation, which, he boasted, entailed nearly one hundred interviews.

But the public was not satisfied by these assurances from law enforcement people, nor would they accept Putnam's plea bargain. All people saw were the obvious indications of premeditated murder: Putnam's flying in and out of Huntington, West Virginia, when he had business in Lexington, Kentucky; Putnam's using a rental car, rather than a government vehicle; Putnam's attempting to conceal the crime, leaving clothing in one place, the trunk mat in another, and so on.

And what seemed to upset the public and Susan's family even more than the handling of the investigation was the outcome of it. Putnam would be eligible for parole after serving just half of his sixteen-year sentence, a sentence which was being served at The Federal Medical Center in Rochester, Minnesota, a low-security place with an almost "country-club" atmosphere.

Meanwhile, John Paul Runyon was busy defending his reputation to the people of Kentucky. Appearing on the WLEX-TV show "Your Government," hosted by Sue Wiley, a popular local news figure, Runyon was answering questions put forth by a panel of newsmen who did not understand why he had worked out a plea with Putnam in such secrecy, and by using such unorthodox methods.

"The three weeks of negotiations were extremely sensitive and delicate. I'm sincere and honest when I say that I didn't know from day to day whether I was going to be talking to them the next day,"

Runyon told the reporters. "There was no reason to involve the family and get them all upset about something they didn't understand.

"Sure, it's unusual to work out a plea prior to the point of indictment," Runyon explained to the panel, "but I don't know of many people who come into my office and say, 'Look, I'm a criminal, I violated the law, and I want to be sent to the penitentiary.' " Runyon went on to express his strong surprise that anyone would so freely confess to such a brutal crime.

"He thought we had more than we did," he continued. "We didn't have anything, but he wasn't sure about that. And I firmly believe this man pled guilty, ultimately, because he wanted to have a clear conscience. There's no other reason." Runyon stared straight into the camera, saying, "This is one of the few cases I know of where a man's conscience led him to confess."

Before the show ended, Runyon was asked if Putnam had been given preferential treatment as an FBI agent, and his response was, "I probably would have gone a little easier on John Q. Public, because this boy was in a position of trust, an official, an officer of the law, and it's my position, if you hold a high position, you pay a higher price for an impropriety . . . but obviously he wasn't going to take the maximum penalty when we had nothing on him."

It was some months before anyone in law enforcement commented on the case again. Most of the involved parties were no longer interested in talking about something over which they no longer had control. Certainly, no one wanted to admit to having done a sloppy job. However, upon reflection, the Putnam confession and plea bargain seemed to bother certain law-enforcement people.

When asked about the incident months after the fact, even KSP Major Jerry Lovitt began to poke holes in Putnam's story and credibility.

"His using a rental car was a chance for more evidence to get away," Lovitt explained. "And Harmon's Branch, that's such a remote area it could have been a natural grave . . . And the fact that he says he hauled that body back across Kentucky, can you imagine? Here's a guy, a college graduate, having worked numerous homicides. People, after they commit the act, go out and do crazy unexplained things, and that's a crazy thing to do, to leave her in a parking lot in Lexington. For one thing, the body's not going to look very pretty. He could have thrown that into the confession, to make himself look like a distressed lover.

"My hypothesis is, killing her may have come into his mind before, and I believe it was a consideration before he came up here," Lovitt finally concluded. "I think he was going to try and reconcile it out, but I think he had made up his mind that he was going to take care of the problem while he was back here in Kentucky, one way or the other."

Chapter Fifteen

While the murder of Susan Daniels Smith did not make national headlines, word of her death sent shock waves as far as Hollywood and New York. Tabloid TV shows such as *A Current Affair* and *Inside Edition* covered the incident. On both these shows Putnam was called a disgrace to the FBI and the former agent's identity was concealed due to fear of "jailhouse justice."

Kathy Putnam told *Inside Edition* that she was behind her husband one hundred percent, and she insisted that she still loved Mark.

"The way I see it, his mistake was with sleeping with her. That hurts. But when I got past the hurt, I realized there's a lot more to what he means to me than sex or even friendship. It's being a part of each other. That's what love is all about," Kathy told the TV reporter. "You don't just throw it away, even though something terrible has happened. The biggest hurt is to be without the person."

On *Inside Edition* Kathy Putnam said she could see trouble coming when Susan Smith started to call their home several times a day, but she didn't find out about the affair or the pregnancy until just before Mark confessed.

"Now that I look back on it, he told me a thousand times in a dozen different ways, but I never heard. It wasn't a love affair . . . it was out of a sense of responsibility for her. She could manipulate people, even though they knew they were being manipulated. She came on to him, like 'I've done everything for you, I've loved you for a year and a half, now do this for me.' "

It was on *Inside Edition* that Kathy Putnam said when she first heard about the killing, she was "denying it." She said Mark told her "I'm going to go to prison for this," and insisted to TV cameras, "my husband felt that he owed it to Susan to confess." Kathy professed she was able to stand by Mark because "he was able to come forward and do what's right."

She told the *Inside Edition* reporter that Susan was asking for trouble, that she was threatening Mark, saying, " 'I'm going to your house and I'm going to put that baby in Danielle's arms and I'm going to show her her little bastard brother, show her what her daddy did to me.' "

Mark Putnam also spoke to *Inside Edition* from the Minnesota prison where he now resides. It was his only public statement since his sentencing, and he spoke to a TV reporter over the phone, his person concealed, his voice emanating from a large white tower.

"I just snapped, pure and simple. I just snapped and grabbed hold of her, around her neck, and then I stopped. . . ." Putnam's voice was steady. "I don't know if it was two seconds or two minutes, and then she stopped hitting me. . . ." Putnam's words ended.

Before the *Inside Edition* segment was over, Kathy Putnam had repeatedly insinuated that the death was an accident, that Susan Smith had brought it upon herself. She told the interviewer, "She really wanted to be me. She wanted to be married to Mark. She wanted me out of the picture. She wanted to be an FBI agent's wife, she really did. . . ." A tear rolled down Kathy's cheek as she spoke into the camera.

Shelby Ward also appeared on the two tabloid shows, lambasting the public authorities for letting Mark Putnam get off with a light jail sentence.

Shelby told *A Current Affair* reporters that Susan had had a hard life. When she tried to make sense of her sister's death, all Shelby could say was, "Maybe he did love her at one time. I don't know why he killed her."

Apart from all the television hype, the weapons charge which had been brought against Shelby Ward had now become an issue in Pikeville. Her trial for trying to bring a concealed weapon into court had been set for August 8, 1990. The .38 caliber pistol she'd carried into court was Ike's gun, and it was worth five hundred dollars. Shelby knew he'd be furious if he had to pay legal fees and fines for the offense, as well as run the risk of having his gun confiscated permanently.

She called Runyon not long after Putnam's sentencing in an attempt to see how seriously he intended to press the charge. When Runyon made it clear that she would be prosecuted to the full extent of the law, Shelby offered to soften her comments to the press regarding the way the Commonwealth Attorney's office and the Kentucky State Police had conducted the investigation into her sister's death. In so doing, she hoped such a course of action might influence the outcome of the gun charges.

After some further consultation with Runyon's office the next day, Shelby Jean Ward, sister of the slain Susan Smith, issued statements to the press, calling her past criticism of the Pike County prosecutor and the state police unfair.

"John Paul Runyon has done the best he could do," one newspaper account read. "I think John Paul Runyon is an honest man, in my heart. If it had not been for him and the Kentucky State Police, my sister would still be lying over on that hill."

In Shelby's public apologies, she praised the government agencies. "Now that I have had the opportunity to think about it and to consider everything that was done surrounding the death of my sister, there is no doubt that the best possible result was accomplished," another newspaper account stated.

Some reporters noted that Ward had changed her mind about the plea agreement after she'd watched a television press conference held by the Commonwealth Attorney and Kentucky State Police Captain Gary Rose.

On August 9, 1990, the day after Shelby appeared in court, local newspapers reported that the concealed weapons charge against Shelby Ward would be dropped in six months, provided she had no problem with the law during that period. In addition, all attendant fines were waived and the court agreed to allow the return of weapon in question.

Afterward, Shelby said, "I didn't mean a word of [my apologies], praising the police and Runyon and all that."

Shelby Ward and John Paul Runyon were far from

seeing the last of each other. Amid the media hype and public accusations and apologies, there was the unfinished business of Susan Smith's postmortem exam and burial. A few days after her public apology, Shelby Ward called John Paul Runyon to ask that Susan's remains be sent back to Freeburn so there could be a funeral. This was a call Runyon may very well have been praying for—evidently he needed an excuse to get Susan Daniels Smith buried and forgotten—but Shelby's call started a chain reaction which upset public officials all over Kentucky.

On Friday afternoon, just days after Putnam was sentenced, Commonwealth Assistant Attorney Rick Bartley called the state medical examiner's office in Frankfort to tell Dr. David Wolfe that the family of Susan Smith wanted him to release the remains without completing the postmortem.

In response to this unusual request Dr. Wolfe called John Paul Runyon directly.

Wolfe said that usually in these kinds of cases, when the family wants the body back for a funeral, he explains to them that it takes weeks to go through the evidence to determine the cause of death. He tells people to hold a memorial service, but he makes them understand the importance of the postmortem procedure.

"I told Runyon I would be happy to talk to the family and explain the situation to them. I said I wasn't trying to prevent them from having a funeral," Wolfe explained. "I've been doing forensic work in Kentucky since 1977, and I belong to the American Academy of Forensic Sciences. I know people from agencies all around the country, but I can't think of any case in which an autopsy or postmortem has been halted in the case of a homicide."

Wolfe told the Commonwealth that he returned from Harmon's Branch with eight twelve-gallon buckets of material, which had to be washed, screened, and dried before the postmortem could get underway. Soil had to be examined for trace evidence, bones had to be put back together to determine whether the fractures were perimortem or postmortem, fingernails, small bones, loose teeth — all had to be sorted through. Moreover, a fetal skeleton was yet to be identified.

Along with this material, Susan's jawbone was found missing two teeth. Later, the forensic examination would suggest that these teeth could have been knocked out at the time of her death.

However, while Wolfe was at the University of Kentucky lab on Friday, June 16, 1990, a call came into his office from the Commonwealth Assistant Attorney Rick Bartley. Bartley allegedly told David Jones, the administrator of the medical examiner's office, that he'd get a "court order" to release Smith's remains if Wolfe did not do so immediately. According to Jones, Bartley threatened to have Wolfe thrown in jail for contempt of court unless the remains were returned to the family at once.

When he returned to his office in Frankfort that day, an enraged Dr. Wolfe got on the phone with John Paul Runyon.

"I'd like to see you try to put me in jail for doing my job," Wolfe said.

"No, no, David Jones misunderstood," Runyon said. "There's no court order. The family just wants the body released."

"Well, there's no good reason to do this in a hurry, because undoubtedly there's going to be a lawsuit, and these questions must be answered."

"Putnam's already pleaded guilty, so there's no use in prolonging this thing," Runyon told him.

"You can't even prove what he's pleaded guilty to actually happened. You don't even know that he killed her at this point," Wolfe argued.

But his protests were of no use. Runyon insisted the remains be returned. Rick Bartley called several times that day, telling Wolfe a judge in Pikeville had said there was no legal reason to continue the postmortem. He also claimed that the coroner's office wanted the remains released to satisfy Smith's family.

Confounded, Wolfe called the Chief Medical Examiner in Louisville and made him aware of what was going on. If the Pike County coroner no longer wanted a postmortem, Wolfe's supervisor felt, "the remains might as well be released . . . the legal questions having been answered and Putnam being behind bars."

But Wolfe believed Putnam was lying in his sworn statement, and he pulled out a copy and went over the testimony again and again, looking for inconsistencies.

He found that a number of statements Putnam had made didn't jibe. On page three, Putnam stated that Susan was hitting him about the face, but Putnam had had no scratches or bruises on his face; eye witnesses attested to that. Wolfe wanted the chance to check Smith's fingernails for remnants of facial tissue. And there was the matter of the cracked windshield. Wolfe did not believe Putnam's contention that Smith could crack safety glass with her bare feet. If she had, there would be trauma to her bones, but now he wasn't even being given a chance to check on that.

And there were other falsehoods in the sworn confession, Wolfe noted. The idea that Putnam "laid" Susan on her back was ludicrous, as was his claim that he'd kept Susan's body in the car for over twelve hours.

"Putnam says he placed her on her back. There's no way he could have placed her. I was at the site on Harmon's Branch. The only way she could have gotten to the bottom of that hill was for him to pitch her over the hillside. The only reason she stopped where she did was she got hung up in a pile of old fencing there, otherwise she would have rolled all the way to the bottom," Wolfe surmised.

Wolfe studied the video of Harmon's Branch made on the day Susan Smith's body was excavated. Putnam said he'd carried Susan down the hill gently, but Wolfe could find only one steep pathway, used by dirt bikes, that Putnam might possibly have traveled. Even this was too steep for anyone to walk down, let alone someone who was carrying a body.

"A dead person weighs a whole lot more than a live person. It's like picking up a sack of lard," Wolfe would later say. "Plus, after a period of time, about three hours, rigor mortis sets in, the body gets stiff. Once rigor sets in, it would take two or three people to lift a body, especially if it's stuffed into the trunk of a car."

Furthermore Wolfe was convinced that Putnam hadn't driven around with Susan in the trunk. He was sure the former FBI agent was a far darker figure than the media or the FBI had made him out to be. Putnam was playing Mr. Nice Guy with the public, but his act wasn't taking Wolfe in.

He said he kissed her on the cheek. Wolfe thought, this happened in June, and if he'd had the body in the trunk of the car, decomposition was well under way. I've seen too many bodies locked in trunks of cars in the summertime, and the odor would never let anyone get near.

Yet Runyon insisted that the postmortem be discontinued, claiming that it was for the sake of Susan Smith's family, so the next day, Wolfe decided to release Susan Smith's remains, albeit under protest, and after having been misled, he claims, by the Commonwealth Attorney.

The next day, editorials and newspaper reports appeared with the headlines: NO AUTOPSY FOR WOMAN SLAIN BY FORMER F.B.I. AGENT.

"In thirteen years of performing autopsies for the state, this is the first time in over 700 cases that I have been told not to fulfill my duty in determining the cause and manner of death," Wolfe told reporters. He also noted that he operated under an annual budget of one and four-tenths million dollars and said the Kentucky medical examiner's office performed twenty-two hundred autopsies in 1990.

"I don't feel that anyone, including the pathologist, has the right to keep the remains just to satisfy scientific curiosity when the family wants the body back," Runyon publicly retorted.

"My interpretation of what happened is this," Wolfe later concluded, "in cases where the normal procedures aren't followed, there's usually a reason why they're not followed. There's usually something to hide. That's been my experience."

Even before the halting of the postmorten became an issue, David Wolfe had been thwarted by the FBI and state police in his attempts to get at the truth behind Susan Smith's death. For instance, he'd asked to be taken to the site where Putnam supposedly killed Smith, Peter Creek Mountain, so he could look for trace evidence, but he was told there would be no point in it; the FBI would be coming in to do a thorough investigation. To Wolfe's knowledge, the FBI never did. Wolfe also asked to see the rental vehicle Putnam had used, but was told FBI officials had already gone through it, and had found nothing in it.

In the meantime, once the Commonwealth got Wolfe to agree to release the remains, the Pike County coroner, Charles Morris, was asked by the Commonwealth to go to Frankfort immediately to pick up the remains, having been led to believe that the postmortem had already been completed.

"I was out of town when all this was going on," Morris said, "and I get a call from the Commonwealth's office when I was on the other side of the state. They were telling me to get to the medical examiner's office and bring the remains back to Phelps, giving me the impression that all the work was finished, that they had finished the examination on Susan Smith."

When Morris arrived in Frankfort it was already after five P.M. so the coroner had to get the security guard to let him into the medical examiner's office. Morris signed a release form and brought Susan Smith's remains straight to the Phelps Funeral Home, leaving the cardboard box with Alice Mullins, the proprietor.

It wasn't until the next day that Charles Morris and David Wolfe spoke to each other and discovered that they both had been duped by the Commonwealth Attorney's office. Wolfe told Morris that he hadn't completed the exam, and Morris told Wolfe that he hadn't requested that the exam be halted. Afterward, Charles Morris refused to sign the death certificate, and although he was being pressured by the Commonwealth, he did not give in.

Susan Smith's remains were being readied for burial. John Paul Runyon had even driven to the Phelps Funeral Home to help Shelby pick out a coffin. The state was paying five hundred dollars for the funeral because the family was too poor to afford a proper burial. The coffin Runyon picked out was child sized, which wasn't the original plan, Shelby claims, but Runyon told her that a full-sized coffin wasn't necessary.

Then two days before the funeral was scheduled, Charles Morris got John Paul Runyon on the phone. He wanted the prosecutor to agree to set up a meeting with Shelby.

"I can't see why, if you've already plea-bargained this thing, you'd want the autopsy halted," Morris told Runyon. "We've never stopped an autopsy for a family before. I've talked to other medical examiners in the state, and they've never heard of anything like this. How can you let a murder case go unanswered?"

Runyon agreed to the meeting, and Shelby Ward and Charles Morris sat down with him later that day. After a brief conversation, the three parties decided to hold off on the funeral to allow Dr. Wolfe to complete the postmortem. Shelby's attorney, Larry Webster, had advised her that a postmortem could affect the results of the three-hundred-twenty-five-thousand-dollar claim the family had filed against the FBI on the grounds that the agency had been negligent by failing to protect Susan Smith from her killer. If the postmortem could show, for instance, that Susan had been beaten to death, the family might be able to collect an even larger amount.

It was agreed on Monday, June 18, that Susan Smith's remains would be sent back to Frankfort. Morris had already seen the remains, and he had questions — about two missing teeth and about the cause of death.

At four P.M. that afternoon, the Pike County coroner received a call from Runyon and was informed that Susan Smith's remains weren't going to be taken back to Frankfort, after all, that the burial was to go on as scheduled.

"Runyon just said there wasn't any point in it. Everything was over and done with," Morris recalls. "I told him I couldn't finish my paperwork without proof of the cause of death, but Runyon refused to listen."

Shelby Ward got a call later that same afternoon from Commonwealth Assistant Attorney Rick Bartley. Bartley told her that the medical examiner's office was refusing to take the remains back because the matter had become a civil one; it was no longer a state case. Bartley explained that the only way a postmortem could be done at this point was for the family to pay for the exam.

"Bartley told me that the autopsy would run into thousands of dollars. He knew I didn't have that kind of money," Shelby said. "I later found out that a private autopsy wouldn't cost nearly as much as they led me to believe."

Shelby continued to push for the completion of the postmortem, but the Commonwealth convinced her that the results wouldn't affect her civil suit, that Susan's death most likely happened the way Putnam said it had, and that Putnam had had no reason to lie about how he killed Susan. By the end of the conversation, the Commonwealth had Shelby convinced that a quick funeral was the best solution.

The next morning, funeral director Alice Mullins, a family friend of the Runyons, contacted Shelby and said, "How about a one-day service? You all come up tonight and have cake and coffee, and we bury tomorrow at one o'clock." Shelby agreed to Alice's plan, even though it seemed so rushed. Carla didn't have time to fly in from Texas, and people didn't have time to send flowers; everything was done in such a big hurry.

Susan Daniels Smith was laid to rest on June 20, 1990, on a small hillside behind her grandfather's house, in the Eldridge family cemetery at Barrenshea Creek. Her brother, Billy Joe, paid a boy twenty-five dollars to clear a plot in this lonely spot where Susan would remain buried for the next few months. There was no tombstone for her, just a plastic copper-tone plaque which listed her name, date of birth, and date of death.

But the entanglement with the FBI was not yet over for Susan Daniels Smith and the members of her family, because not long after her burial, Shelby and Billy Joe were called and asked to talk to FBI agents as part of the ongoing FBI internal investigation of Mark

Putnam. They were questioned for over two hours in the Pikeville FBI office in mid July, 1990.

"When Sarah Pickard of the FBI called me and asked if I would talk, I insisted on having my attorney with me, and when we got there, she was very nice. She had an FBI man from Nashville—Agent Raymond Eganey, Jr.—with her, and she introduced us. Huggins was there, and he said they knew I'd been through a lot, and they were apologizing, not for Mark but on their own behalf," Shelby recalls.

Handled by the FBI's Office of Professional Responsibility, the questioning centered on two agents—Terry Hulse, Putnam's former supervisor, and Ron Poole, Putnam's former partner.

The FBI team interrogated Shelby about Susan's pregnancy, wanting to know how much Ron Poole knew about that and the affair. Shelby insisted that Ron had been fully aware of what was going on, and she said Terry Hulse was also aware of the problem. Shelby told the FBI team that according to Ron Poole, Hulse had walked into the Pikeville office at one point and, looking at Mark, had said, "I heard you're going to be a daddy. I heard you're going to have a little papoose." But Mark and Ron had just laughed the remark off.

During the two hours of tape-recorded conversation Shelby had with the FBI agents, some of the talk also centered on Putnam's alleged pilfering of cocaine from the FBI evidence safe. Shelby repeated what she had heard Susan say about that. She also told the FBI investigators all about the "party" Ron and Mark had the day Susan went over to their office with her friend Donna Charles, who allegedly lifted her blouse.

"Their eyes bugged out when I said that," Shelby said, "and they were writing things down, looking at each other like they couldn't believe it."

While Shelby was in with Agents Pickard and Eganey, Billy Joe was being questioned in a separate room by Jim Huggins.

"Poole was bragging about how he cracked the case," Billy Joe said. "He told me he'd like to come to Freeburn to express his sympathy to the family, but I told him it wouldn't be a good idea."

When the issue of witness protection came up, Huggins told Billy Joe that whatever Putnam had told Susan must have been a total misstatement. Apparently Putnam had had Susan believing that once someone goes under witness protection, no one in the world knows the whereabouts of that person, not even family members. But Huggins informed Billy Joe Daniels that the witness protection system didn't work that way, that at least one family member is told where the person under protection is.

When Ron Poole's name came up again, Billy Joe talked about the day he and Ron went out to Josie Thorpe's and Helen Prater's to check on the phone calls from a "Susan Smith."

"Ron told me he was sick of Mark playing these little games," Billy Joe told Huggins. "He was mad because Putnam was making him look awful bad."

The results of the internal FBI probe have never been made public. There are newspaper reporters threatening to seek access under the Freedom of Information Act, for access to the report, but no action has been taken by any member of the press to date.

Epilogue

About three months after Putnam's sentencing, an employee of the Goldenrod Motel, Cleo Burgess, came forward with information about the former FBI agent's stays there. The Kentucky State Police went to the Goldenrod and found that records indeed showed that Putnam stayed at the Goldenrod eight or nine times from August through December of 1988. Each time, a woman who matched the description of Susan Smith was seen waiting out in Putnam's brown car as Putnam went into the office and identified himself, saying he needed to question someone in the room. He sometimes paid for one person, twenty-two dollars and five cents; at other times motel employees insisted that he pay for two persons, twenty-three dollars and ten cents.

After he and the woman would leave, said Goldenrod employee Connie Haynes, the chambermaid would find one bed "messed up" along with some dirty towels. Another Goldenrod employee, Mageline Hall, told police that Mark Putnam came back to the hotel "around the first of

1989," wanting some receipts. Evidently, at that time, Putnam threw his FBI badge down on the front desk and demanded his "sign in" cards. Putnam was told the cards were kept by the motel owner, Katie Malik, who was not available. He left in a rage, without his registration cards, and never returned to the Goldenrod again.

Agent Ron Poole stopped calling Shelby Ward in July, 1990, about four weeks after Susan Smith was buried, telling her that he had been transferred to Lexington, although he remained assigned to the Pikeville office well into 1991. Shelby alleges that throughout the missing-person investigation, Poole called her many times a day, often trying to "come on" to her, asking what kind of panties she had on, whether she was tan—questions of that nature—and telling Shelby he was going to leave his wife. Poole did file for divorce on April 2, 1990, Pike Circuit Court records show, but that action was never completed and Poole continues to reside with his wife, Cynthia, and their three children.

On July 31, 1990, Pikeville attorney Larry Webster filed an administrative claim with the FBI in Washington, alleging that the FBI's negligence "was a proximate cause in the death of Susan Smith" and asserting that both of Putnam's co-workers should have realized that Putnam was under "an extreme amount of pressure and subject to carry out some untoward act upon learning of the pregnancy. . . ."

Webster claims that both Hulse and Poole were negligent in failing to see that the relationship between Smith and Putnam was terminated, failing to take steps to protect Smith from the consequences of that relationship, and failing to see that Smith received personal protection. The administrative claim against the FBI has not been acted upon to date. Consequently, there is no formal suit pending against the FBI involving Susan Daniels Smith.

In April, 1991, a Pike County judge granted a request by Susan Smith's family to exhume her remains. The exhumation took place on May 20, 1991, at nine A.M., at which time Susan Smith's remains were transported to the office of Dr. David Wolfe so that a postmortem could be done. Mark Putnam hired a Louisville attorney, who appointed Anthony Perzigian, a forensic anthropologist and Associate Dean at the University of Cincinnati, to look over Wolfe's shoulder. Perzigian went to Frankfort on two different occasions, at which times he witnessed Wolfe's examination and was involved in some analysis of Susan Smith's remains. Both men found evidence of some sort of struggle. Specifically, they discovered the right styloid—a bone projection at the temple—was broken around the time of Susan's death. Wolfe also discovered a small fracture to the right nasal bone, a perimortem fracture which occurred just prior to death.

Wolfe points out that his findings do not indicate that Susan died of strangulation, and he says he cannot prove the method of death because the thyroid cartilage, which would have to be examined, is missing from Susan Smith's remains. Wolfe says the broken styloid bone indicates that Susan could have been killed by a blow to the head.

Upon further inspection of Susan Smith's remains, David Wolfe discovered a number of discrepancies, the most significant being that the material returned to him was incomplete. Three bags of debris had been stapled shut; debris which should have contained the fetal tissue and Susan Smith's missing teeth was now gone. As a result, Wolfe has been unable to locate any trace of fetal tissue.

Moreover, Wolfe says sixteen grams of "soft tissue" connected to a leg bone left his office, but when the remains came back, the soft tissue — muscle — connected to the bone weighed only four and a half grams. Wolfe says when he sent the sixteen grams of soft tissue to Phelps, it was in a separate box sealed with evidence tape, and that the box is also missing.

Upon the return of Susan Smith's remains, Wolfe discovered trace evidence — some torn fingernails with soft tissue adhering to them — and he is suggesting a court order might be obtained for Mark Putnam to submit to a DNA analysis to see if the soft tissue under Smith's nails is indeed his. Wolfe says he believes it is possible that more than one person participated in the death of Susan Smith.

He discovered red fibers in the debris. According to Putnam's confession Susan Smith was wearing gray, not red. The fibers might have come from the interior of the rental car, but according to Wolfe, "The FBI has not been forthcoming about divulging the color of the interior of the car."

As it stands now, Dr. David Wolfe can only file an incomplete report on Susan Daniels Smith.

Handwriting experts have now been called in to analyze the signature on the positive pregnancy result slip Susan supposedly signed. Wolfe has pointed out that no other documents, specifically no lab results, have been produced by the Pike County Health Department to prove that Susan Smith was ever pregnant. He says it's possible someone filled in the pregnancy-test authorization form, signing Susan Smith's name, in a "cover-up" effort, although Shelby Ward says that Susan did, in fact, sign the pregnancy-result slip.

On August 27, 1991, Alice (Mullins) Eldridge of the Phelps Funeral Home wrote a notarized statement in which she explained to David Wolfe that on June 14, 1990, she was told to "hold up" Susan Smith's funeral by Commonwealth Assistant Attorney Rick Bartley. Bartley then called her on June 17 and told her to have the funeral. The funeral director wrote that she received Susan Smith's remains in a cardboard box, and she also received a box containing fingernails painted red, a wisp of hair, a gold cross, and some dirt. She made no mention of receiving the three stapled packages which contained Susan's small bones. In these the fetal bones would be found.

"All the above mentioned were placed in the casket, which was wired shut," she wrote. "I did not examine the skeletal remains."

"She doesn't say whether the remains were sealed or unsealed when she put them in the casket," Wolfe points out, "or where the cardboard box was or who had access to it between June 13 and June 19, 1990."

If the forensic anthropologist had been able to uncover enough evidence, Mark Putnam might have been retried in a federal court for murdering a federal witness. Instead, perhaps Susan Smith's murder, tricky and well plotted, will remain forever unsolved.

Author's Note

Mark Steven Putnam was twice contacted in writing, both in jail and through his attorney, but did not make any attempt to cooperate with this project.

Kathy Putnam was likewise contacted in writing, but did not respond in any way.

Special Agent Ronald Poole was contacted in writing and in person, but said he could not discuss anything regarding the Mark Putnam case.

Pike County Commonwealth Attorney John Paul Runyon was contacted both in writing and on the telephone, but repeatedly refused to cooperate.

J. Kevin O'Brien, chief, Freedom of Information, US Department of Justice, logged a request for the file on this case in March 1991, but due to the delay encountered in processing, his office has not been forthcoming with the information.

A.J.